Birds of the Upper Mississippi River and Driftless Area

An Anthology of Stories From Big River Magazine

Edited by Pamela Eyden,

Molly McGuire

and Reggie McLeod

Photographs by Alan Stankevitz

All of the stories in *Birds of the Upper Mississippi River and Driftless Area* have appeared previously in *Big River Magazine.*

ISBN 978-0-9653950-8-3

Published by
Big River
P.O. Box 204
Winona, MN 55987
1-800-303-8201

Big River Magazine publishes stories and news about the Upper Mississippi River and the Driftless Area.

www.bigrivermagazine.com

Introduction

Birds have always held a supernatural fascination for us earth-bound humans. They can fly so high as to disappear. They can dive through the air at 70 mph. They can fly underwater. Hide on the ground in plain sight. Float in the air as if weightless. They migrate thousands of miles back and forth every year. And, we very much enjoy watching and learning about them.

That's one reason stories about birds appear more frequently in *Big River Magazine* than stories about fish, mammals or insects. Readers seem to be equally interested in our flighty neighbors.

When we began compiling stories for what we intend to be a series of anthologies, birds were a natural first focus. These stories were written over a period of 22 years; the publication date is on each story's title page. Except in cases where someone referenced or quoted in the story has switched jobs, retired or died, the facts have not changed. Threatened birds are still a concern and the returned eagles, pelicans, cormorants and others are still going about their lives.

About our contributors: writer Pamela Eyden, who wrote most of these stories, has had a crucial role in *Big River* since it started, in 1993. She wrote many of the best stories that appeared in the magazine, bird stories as well as memorable stories about frogs, bears, ice boats and many other subjects. She is currently *Big River*'s editor-at-large.

Molly McGuire has been with *Big River* nearly as long, working at nearly every task, from bookkeeping to writing. She is *Big River*'s managing editor and is responsible for the layout and design of the magazine, as well as for this book.

Local photographer Alan Stankevitz generously gave us access to his incredible catalog of bird photographs, most of which were taken on or near the Upper Mississippi River. His photos have graced so many covers of *Big River* that they have become part of the magazine's image.

The stories here have not been updated. For ongoing information about birds in the Driftless Area and the changes affecting them and their habitats, read *Big River Magazine*.

Personally, I have really enjoyed reading all of these stories again and getting back in touch with writers I haven't talked to for awhile.

Green herons, vultures, kingfishers, crows, eagles, pelicans and the other birds are all amazing neighbors in this beautiful place we are blessed to live in. I also feel very blessed to have worked with so many talented and interesting human beings.

I hope you enjoy these stories and photographs as much as I have, and I hope they increase your enjoyment of the rivers, valleys and blufftops of the Driftless Area.

Reggie McLeod, *Big River Magazine* editor/publisher

Table of Contents

Backwater Birds

Belted Kingfishers 3
By Pamela Eyden

Great Blue Herons 7
By Pamela Eyden

Great Egrets — Exotic Natives 11
By Pamela Eyden

Sunrise in a Wetland Counting Cranes 17
By Pamela Eyden

Blackbirds of a Feather Flock Together 21
By Pamela Eyden

A Crazy Heron with a Tackle Box 27
By Pamela Eyden

Bluffland Birds

Scrappy Eagles on a Blue Water Day 33
By Sally Sloan

Peregrines Return 37
By Pamela Eyden

A Good Year for Falcons 39
By Pamela Eyden

Back to the Bluffs 43
By Fran Howard

Turkey Vultures — Beautiful, from a Distance 47
By Pamela Eyden

Living with a Vulture 51
By Joan Schnabel

Forest Birds

Haunts of the Red-headed Woodpecker..57
By Thomas V. Lerczak

Frog Hawks and Chicken Hawks 61
By Pamela Eyden

Winter Owls..65
By Joan Schnabel

Turning No-Man's-Land into a Nature Preserve 71
By Pamela Eyden

Main Channel Birds

American White Pelicans Stage a Comeback....................................79
By Pamela Eyden

Listen for These White Swans' Songs...83
By Molly McGuire

Mallards — Adaptable Dabblers, Drakes in Drag...........................89
By Pamela Eyden

Cormorant Wars 93
By Pamela Eyden

Looking Just Ducky..99
By Pamela Eyden and Reggie McLeod

Birds Found Everywhere

Crows — Smart and Playful..107
By Joan Schnabel

Nighthawk Twilight 111
By Molly McGuire

Cooper's Hawks 117
By Joan Schnabel

Kestrels — Little Raptors with a Big Attitude 121
By Joan Schnabel

Swallows of the Upper Mississippi 125
By Thomas V. Lerczak

Seasons of Birding

Waves of Waterfowl 133
By Pamela Eyden

Birding in Winter 139
By Pamela Eyden

Eavesdrop on the Owls of Winter 147
By Joan Schnabel

Birds in January 151
By Pamela Eyden

Birds in February 153
By Pamela Eyden

Birds in March 157
By Pamela Eyden

Birds in April 159
By Pamela Eyden

Birds in May 163
By Pamela Eyden

Paddling for Birds on the Mississippi 165
By Tom Watson

Favorite Fall Birding Spots on the Upper Mississippi 171
By Pamela Eyden

Bird Science

Cruising for a Bird's Eye View of Ducks, Geese and Swans 181
By Pamela Eyden

Soaring with the Dinosaurs — Young eagles remind us of the
evolution of flight 187
By Robert E. Sloan

National Birdhood: Eagle? Or Turkey? 193
By Marc Hequet

Contributors 196

Index 197

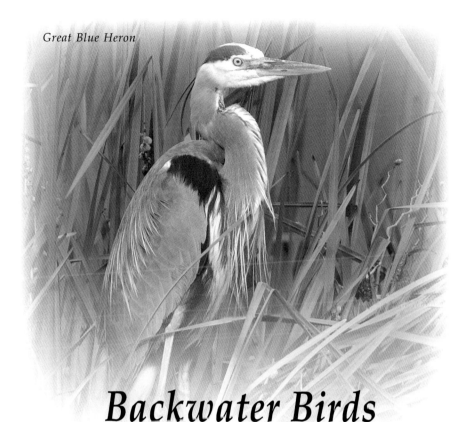

Great Blue Heron

Backwater Birds

Belted Kingfishers 3

Great Blue Herons 7

Great Egrets — Exotic Natives................................... 11

Sunrise in a Wetland Counting Cranes 17

Blackbirds of a Feather Flock Together 21

A Crazy Heron with a Tackle Box 27

Belted kingfisher

Belted Kingfishers

By Pamela Eyden

I n March and April everything seems to happen at once. Ice melts. Waters rise. Algae bobs to the surface. Fish move to their spawning grounds. Turtles and frogs emerge from the mud. Bugs climb toward new buds at the ends of twigs. Sap rises. Birds return.

If you knew a quarter of what was going on, you'd probably snuggle back under your winter quilt for a rest. Instead, you take a walk across a bridge, down a path, next to a backwater channel or a pond. If you watch with an inquiring mind, you may see common birds do some unusual things.

Take the belted kingfisher, for example. This bird is easy to identify any time of year. It has a big head, a jagged crest and a blue swag across its white chest. It perches in conspicuous places and dives headfirst into the water to catch fish. In early spring, kingfishers' vivid blue feathers are the brightest thing in the backwaters.

The U.S. Geological Survey Northern Prairie Research Center marks April 25 as the average peak of belted kingfisher migration through central Minnesota and Wisconsin. Some birds return from as far south as central and northern South America, and may continue on into Canada. Males arrive first. They don't migrate as far as females, and they may not migrate at all if there is enough open water to catch fish all winter. Once back they have to be quick. A few days makes a lot of difference in whether they become successful parents.

With aerial combat and raucous, rattling cries, belted kingfishers will fight over the best territories, such as 1,000 feet of shoreline with rippled water where fish tend to gather and varied habitat to support other possible prey, such as crayfish, frogs, tadpoles, insects and even mice.

"There's a little backwater pool on the Mississippi up here [near St. Cloud, Minn.] that kingfishers come to early in the spring, because snowmelt causes high water other places," said Jim Davis. Davis studied belted kingfishers for many years before and after getting his Ph.D. in zoology, focussing on animal communication and behavior.

"Kingfishers need shallow water. They don't really swim after the fish. They can only catch them a few inches below the surface, and they close their protective eye membranes as they enter the water, so they don't see far. Those membranes are hardly translucent." Kingfishers can only seize fish that are a maximum of three inches long, although this depends on the type of fish — a three-inch-long sunfish might be too wide to swallow.

When the female arrives, she returns to her old nest area and checks out the resident male. This may or may not be the same one she mated with the year before. Nest site fidelity, not mate fidelity, is the rule for belted kingfishers, according to Davis. One bird he banded in Ohio returned to the same site five years in a row. The female stays if the resident male is persuasive and healthy, and if he courts her with fish.

Early spring observers may see this courtship feeding ritual, Davis said. The male bird catches fish and returns to a conspicuous perch to feed the female. He may do this many times, thus proving he's a competent fisher in a productive territory.

These birds are unusual in that females are more colorful than males, sporting a wide rufous-red band below the blue on their chests. Some researchers think that this reversal in the usual coloration may be part of a larger pattern of sex role reversal.

"It's my feeling, from research I've done on territorial behavior and vocalizations, that females are more aggressive than males, and males are more domestic," said Davis. While both sexes defend their nesting and fishing territory, females seem to react more quickly and fiercely to invaders. Males take more responsibility for raising the young than do most birds.

After courtship, the pair selects a nest site, usually on a vertical bank of compacted sandy soil clear of brush and vegetation. Starting a foot or two below the top of the bank, they dig an eight-foot-long tunnel that slants upward, using their bills as chisels and their feet to push the debris out behind them. Tunnel openings are three or four inches wide, with telltale grooves where birds scrape their toes when they land. The location discourages snakes, raccoons and other predators.

According to Davis, "Ownership of suitable nesting banks are hotly contested each spring, with males battling males and females battling females."

Like all their relatives in the order *coraciiformes*, belted kingfishers are very vocal birds. "They have a lot of interesting vocalizations that would be very hard to describe in a publication," he said.

Kingfishers generally raise one brood a year, containing an average of seven eggs. Young kingfishers are initially fed small pieces of pre-digested fish. Later the birds demand about 12 fish each per day.

"That's a lot of fishing!" said Davis, who cautioned that his study was in Ohio, and there may be some variation in other places.

After receiving his Ph.D. and doing postdoctoral studies with the Smithsonian Institution in Panama, Davis taught for a while, but eventually decided to leave academia. He now runs his own business, Interpretive Birding, which is part web page and part monthly bulletin devoted to interpreting bird behavior. He also leads birding tours, in which participants agree to focus on birds' behaviors, not their identities.

"Birding today is dominated by the 'list' mentality, which is not very intellectually exciting," he said. "Asking questions about what birds are doing and why livens up the activity. Even if you see the same birds, there is always new behavior."

Davis and a friend developed their ideas about interpretive birding while they were in Australia. "We had seen just about all the birds there were to see, except for the most rare ones," Davis said. "Then one day we watched an olive-backed oriole mimicking a bird that is its nest predator. We had lively debates about why it would do that."

Great blue herons

Great Blue Herons

By Pamela Eyden

One afternoon many years ago, I was walking on an island up north when I heard a series of guttural screams and cries that rooted me to the spot. It sounded like a battle of giant lizards. I crept cautiously through the woods until I came to the edge of a clearing and peered up into the treetops at a colony of — what? — pterodactyls? I counted the nests, sketched the birds as best I could and hurried home to call the University of Minnesota with my discovery.

"Oh, yes," said the woman at the Bell Museum, "they're great blue herons. We know that rookery."

Great blue herons? It never occurred to me that the raucous, clumsy, screaming, quarrelsome creatures in the treetops were the same bird as the solitary, elegant, ethereal blue heron.

The great blue heron (*Ardea herodias*) truly is a bird of many contrasts; standing four feet tall with a wingspan of six feet, it is one of the continent's largest birds, yet it can stand so still as to seem nearly invisible. It's a water-wader who nests in the tops of tall trees. It's a solitary hunter who raises its young in a crowded colony.

Herons are easy to identify and rewarding to watch, especially in the spring and early summer, when adults are at the peak of their beauty. Although the female is smaller and a paler blue than the male,

Big River Magazine, April 1998

both grow the long head feathers that are a trademark of their kind.

Envy and desire for the extravagant plumes of the great blue heron and its cousin, the egret, drove an international market at the turn of the century. Military costumers and high-fashion haberdashers pounced on the fabulous feathers, which sold for $32 per ounce. In 1902, at a single auction, 3,000 pounds of heron and egret plumes were sold, with about $1,536,000 changing hands over the remains of 200,000 birds.

Protective laws were passed and the Audubon Society was formed out of the public outcry over the near extinction of egrets and herons.

Colonial Life

It's not unusual for hundreds, even thousands, of herons to nest together in a colony. The nests are crude-looking assemblages of sticks and twigs several feet across in the canopy of tall trees — sometimes 60 to 100 feet off the ground.

"You could follow your nose to a rookery if you wanted to, but I don't know if most people would care to go in there," said La Crosse, Wisconsin, birder Fred Lesher. "Besides the stink and nettles and mosquitoes and poison ivy, the young birds tend to regurgitate their fish dinners when they get alarmed. It's the only place I've ever been rained on by 10-inch bullheads." (If that doesn't work, they turn around and get you with the other end.)

Too many disturbances may cause herons to abandon their nests, so it's best to keep your distance, for the birds' sake if not your own, but there are a few heron colonies that people can observe without disturbing the birds. One, just downstream from the Sabula, Iowa, bridge, can be observed from the road.

Waiting for Dinner

Christine Custer, wildlife biologist with the Upper Mississippi Science Center in La Crosse, monitors the rookeries from a wing-above Cessna, from April through mid-July. The last few years she has studied how far nesting herons fly to feed. She's discovered that while most herons stay less than 10 kilometers (6.2 miles) from the rookery, some fly as far as 60.

"This surprises and amazes me," said Custer. "It's a big investment of energy for a bird to fly that far. And it's not just certain rookeries — each colony has birds flying short and long distances."

It's Mating Season ...

Early in April and May, the first males to arrive move into existing nests and if they haven't found a mate yet, try to attract one. It's a busy time. First of all, they have to defend their nests from other males who try to steal sticks to build their own. Then they have to preen and pose to impress single females. When a female sees a male she likes, she flies in and settles on a nearby branch. The male, playing hard to get (or is he just confused?), often tries to drive her away. If she's still interested, she persists until he changes his mind and invites her onto the nest.

After that there's sometimes a stick-exchange ritual, a 30-second circle flight — the only time herons fly with necks stretched out straight, like cranes — and mutual grooming.

Herons are said to be as meticulous about their grooming as cats. Oil from a special gland on the tail keeps the feathers glossy and water-repellent. But they also have a small, comb-like, serrated hook on the middle talons of their feet that is good for straightening feathers and scratching up the patches of "powderdown" — special feathers that disintegrate easily and serve as a cleaning agent.

Poetically enough, the only place the heron can't groom itself is behind its own head, and this is what mates do for each other to affirm the bond between them. They give up grooming each other when the young are hatched.

Next year they choose a new mate and start all over again.

Custer said great blue herons prefer the backwaters of the Mississippi to its Main Channel. Except for that, they are pretty flexible, willing to fish offshore of a rip-rapped bank or from logs.

Herons' standard fishing technique is to stand and wait, but they will also jump with both feet and dip a wing to startle the fish, if necessary. Herons on the Upper Mississippi don't have it as easy as herons in other parts of the U.S. "It may take them one hour of standing and waiting to catch a big fish, half that to catch a smaller fish," said Custer. "This is a low rate compared to coastal areas."

This summer Custer will fly above heron colonies in the Vermillion River Bottoms, between Hastings and Red Wing, Minn., and at Pigs Eye Island at St. Paul. Pigs Eye Island may be one of the oldest traditional heron colony sites in Minnesota.

"We think it may have been here at the time of the first European explorers," said Joan Galli, regional nongame wildlife specialist for the Minnesota Department of Natural Resources (DNR). "They wrote about seeing a great colony of eagles' nests on that island." Eagles, she points out, don't nest in colonies, although they will take over an unused heron nest sometimes. A heron colony may also include double-crested cormorants, great egrets, black-crowned night-herons, an occasional yellow-crowned night-heron, songbirds and even — the wolf among the sheep — a great horned owl's nest.

Natural Cycles or Problems?

Most colonies last only a few decades. There are currently 17 active rookeries in Mississippi River pools 1 through 14, usually situated on islands and in floodplain forests.

Biologist Eric Nelson of the U.S. Fish and Wildlife Service (USFWS) said it's surprising how quickly a colony can build up and decline. The heron rookery on Beaver Island, near Clinton, Iowa, numbered 1,400 nests (2,800 adult birds) in 1993; last year there were just 36. The rookery on Mertes Slough, near Winona, had 13 nests in 1977, 900 in 1994 and 600 last year.

"There's a fair amount of interchange among nesting colonies," Nelson said, "and no evidence that herons return to the same one every year."

The total number of active nests in pools 4 through 14 has diminished in the last decade or so, from 8,000 nests in 16 colonies in 1989 to 4,800 nests in 14 colonies in 1997.

"There is speculation that loss of foraging habitat — marshes and wetlands — along the Mississippi River may be pushing herons up into the smaller rivers, where they can catch their food more easily," said Nelson.

The heron population along the river today may be smaller than in 1987, but it's still greater than it was in the 1960s, when DDT, PCBs and heavy metals threatened herons and so many other birds.

But that is not all that is happening. According to USFWS records, the size of the average brood has dropped over the past five years, from 2 fledglings per nest in 1994 to 1.7 in 1995, 1.6 in 1996 and 1.4 in 1997. Nelson said this may or may not be the result of a natural population cycle in herons.

Great Egrets — Exotic Natives

By Pamela Eyden

The great egret is one of the most dramatic and photogenic birds of the Upper Mississippi. In fact, its beautiful plumage nearly doomed the species a century ago.

Like its cousin the great blue heron, this long-legged wading bird strides as slowly and deliberately as a tai chi master through the backwaters, stalking fish, snails, frogs and invertebrates. It stretches out its neck to an ungainly length and waits motionless for minutes at a time. Then it strikes lightning fast, tosses its head back and swallows its dinner whole. Hunger satisfied, the egret sits with its shoulders hunched and head pulled in, a brilliant white bird against the green of the backwaters.

Egrets and herons — it's easy to tell the difference on the Upper Mississippi. Great blue herons are gray blue and egrets are white. It's not so simple in other parts of the country. There are 10 species of egrets and herons in North America. Where they all stalk the same shallows they can be hard to tell apart.

The snowy egret, for example, is white and about the same size as

Great egret

the white form of the little blue heron. The regular adult little blue heron is blue, but it looks a lot like the juvenile reddish egret, which is also blue. The adult reddish egret is a vivid ruddy red, yet in some lights one can mistake it for a tricolored heron.

A friend and I once spent all morning distinguishing among 19 heron and egret species at the Ding Darling National Wildlife Refuge in Florida. By the time we left, the only one we hadn't seen was the cattle egret. Five minutes later, a large white bird landed on the hood of the car as we parked at a grocery store. It stepped toward us, curled its toes around the windshield wipers and turned its head to one side and the other, as though presenting its distinguishing features — yellow eyes, orange feet, and a flowing crown and necklace of golden yellow feathers that swayed in the lightest breeze. Voila! The cattle egret.

You don't often get that close to the egrets and herons around here. They may be accustomed to people, but at a distance.

The great egret and the great blue heron are closely related. They are the only two species in the genus *Ardea* of the family *Ardidae*. They are regarded as "white herons," along with the little egret, the snowy egret, the reddish egret, the little blue heron and the cattle egret.

Many egrets are more closely related to other herons than to other egrets.

In the Upper Mississippi the great egret and the great blue heron hunt in the same shallow backwaters and often nest together in tree-top colonies, but they behave differently. For one thing, egrets arrive later and begin nesting a few weeks after herons.

In her research, Christine Custer, wildlife biologist with the U.S. Geological Survey Upper Midwest Environmental Sciences Center in La Crosse, Wis., noted that egrets prefer to land in shallow water, not on logs, snags or rocks, while herons land on logs and snags a substantial percentage of the time. She noted also that egrets are quite willing to land where other egrets and herons are, and they are often found feeding in fairly large congregations. Herons, on the other hand, prefer to land where no other birds are near.

"I think this has to do with how much food is available here in any one spot," Custer said. "In Louisiana and Texas, the wetlands are filthy with fish, and the birds strike much more often. You can imagine that a bird wouldn't hesitate to set down if there is plenty for him and plenty for a buddy." In the South, colonial wading birds fish together. They don't have to defend their fishing spots from intruders.

When Custer tracked egrets and herons from their nesting colonies to their first feeding areas of the day, she found that egrets fly farther to feed than herons do. Plotting their feeding areas relative to their nesting colonies, she found a 20-kilometer radius around each one. The birds you see feeding together in the same area also nest together in the same colonies.

Custer found egrets nesting with herons at only three of the eight colonies she visited. This, she hypothesized, was because of the egret's larger feeding radius. (Custer's research, "Feeding Habitat Characteristics of the Great Blue Heron and Great Egret Nesting Along the Upper Mississippi River 1995-1998," was published in the journal *Waterbirds* in vol. 27, 2004.)

Habitat loss is the single major threat to egrets and herons on the Mississippi River — but the threat is much greater below Rock Island, Ill., where the floodplain has been largely destroyed. Contaminants such as PCBs, mercury, organochlorines and selenium also seem to be less of a problem on the Upper Mississippi than in other areas. Research in 1984 by John Nosek and Ray Faber of Saint Mary's University, and research in 1996 by Thomas Custer, et al., found these substances in the eggshells of both herons and egrets, but with minimal thinning of the shells.

Great blue herons far outnumber egrets on the Upper Mississippi River. Of the 14 total rookeries in river pools 4 to 14, egrets nest in just four, with a total of from 100 to 300 nests, according to Eric Nelson of the U.S. Fish and Wildlife Upper Mississippi River Refuge. The count for great blue herons, on the other hand, is 3,500 to 5,000 nests in 14 rookeries. Small as it is, Nelson said, the egret population seems to be increasing.

Too Popular

In the late 1800s, egrets were driven nearly to extinction by plume hunters eager to supply a growing market. Back when long-haired women wore extravagant hats decorated with bird feathers, heads and bodies, some fancy feathers were actually worth their weight in gold. Hunters searched for colonies of egrets sitting on their nests. It was easy to pick off the birds as they came and went, feeding their young.

Great egret and snowy egret plumes were among the most popular. As egrets' and other birds' populations plummeted, the public outcry grew along with a will to protect the birds. Early Audubon Societies were leading forces in stopping the slaughter of these birds for the millinery trade. On May 25, 1900, the Lacey Act became law, prohibiting game taken illegally in one state from being shipped across state boundaries. After many amendments, the law now covers all fish and wildlife and their parts or products, and plants protected by the Convention on International Trade in Endangered Species and those protected by state law.

In 1903, President Theodore Roosevelt created the nation's first national wildlife refuge on Pelican Island, Fla., whose egret population had been nearly wiped out by the feather trade. Between 1903 and 1909 he created 51 "National Bird Reservations," thus establishing the National Wildlife Refuge system.

National Wildlife Refuges celebrate International Migratory Bird Day on or around the second Saturday in May. May is a month of vast bird migrations in the Upper Mississippi River Valley.

Sandhill cranes

Sunrise in a Wetland Counting Cranes

By Pamela Eyden

One Saturday morning every April, thousands of people in Wisconsin, Illinois, Iowa and Minnesota get up in the middle of the night, pull on their rubber boots and warm jackets, and drive to assigned places near the Mississippi and smaller rivers. They abandon their cars at the edge of the road and walk quietly into the fields and wetlands 30 minutes before sunup, carrying binoculars, maps and clipboards. Here they stand waiting, listening, hoping to rendezvous with sandhill cranes.

Greater sandhill cranes stand 40 to 50 inches tall (102 to 127 mm) and have wingspreads of six to seven feet (1.8 to 2.1 m). They are often mistaken for herons, which are about the same size, but cranes fly with their necks stretched out straight and legs trailing behind. (Herons trail their legs once in a while, but they fly with their necks doubled up. Geese stick their necks out, but tuck in their feet.)

Both genders are gray, with red foreheads, but they have a habit of painting themselves with mud and vegetation, and by the time they arrive in the north in March or April, they may look brown, gold, buff, ocher, rust, charcoal or sandy-colored, camouflaged for the wetlands they build their nests in and for the chicks.

Big River Magazine, April 1999

At sunrise the cranes often start moving from their roosts in the shallow waters of the river into the farm fields nearby. They've learned that one of the best sources of food in early spring is grain leftover from the previous year's harvest, although, as omnivores, they also eat roots, tubers, frogs, fish, crayfish, mice, snakes and snails. As the big birds move around to look for breakfast, they startle each other and trumpet loudly to defend their own territories.

That's when the equally-startled crane watcher marks the location of the call on her or his map. These photocopied maps contain the scribbled notes from all those who've identified birds in the area in years past.

This annual Crane Count is organized by the International Crane Foundation of Baraboo, Wis., to monitor breeding populations of sandhill cranes, one of the largest birds in North America. The volunteer effort relies on thousands of people. Last year, 3,033 people stood watch on 1,679 sites in the four states. The count gets bigger every year, so many of the crane counters are first-timers, recruited by friends or from bird clubs, but there's a high return rate.

"Once people do it, they tend to want to do it again," said Kathleen Carlisle, who has organized the crane counts in Trempealeau County for 18 years. "I think it's the wetland morning experience that draws people back."

Counts are always held on a weekend in mid to late April, when birds defending their territory are likely to be most vocal and demonstrative. Counts begin at 5:30 a.m. and end at 7:30 a.m., because dawn and dusk are the two best times to hear them.

When she first started organizing counts, Kathleen Carlisle said, her crane counters were usually disappointed, because there weren't any cranes in Trempealeau County.

"I had to keep telling people how important their negative data would be, eventually!" Carlisle said.

"Today the cranes have expanded their range so much that most observers return with reports of hearing cranes or seeing them."

Protection of the birds and their wetland habitat nurtured the increase (see sidebar).

Crane counters are most likely to hear the guard call — a short, loud warning call that sounds something like a loon, goose, trumpet or bugle, but wilder. In books, it's written, "Garooooooo!"

The other call is the unison call, which is a duet of mates: the female's two notes in a high register superimposed on the male's

Cranes are Coming Back

Cranes have been on earth longer than any bird still living — 60 million years. Glaciers have covered the continent several times, and thousands of creatures have come and gone since cranes started inventing what it was to be cranes.

Of the 15 species of cranes in the world, seven are endangered.

The sandhill crane species has six subspecies; three are endangered.

The greater sandhill crane subspecies, which ranges from the Great Lakes to the Pacific, has five regional groups. The great birds that return to the Mississippi River Valley and the Upper Midwest every spring are part of the Eastern group. For a while they, too, were endangered.

The Eastern group summers in the Upper Mississippi and Great Lakes area, and winters in Florida and the Texas Gulf Coast. Those that winter in Texas migrate north by way of the Mississippi River Flyway. (They can fly 300 miles in a day, and they make good time in the spring, when they are all strong adults.)

Records show that greater sandhill cranes had disappeared from Illinois by 1890, Iowa by 1905, South Dakota by 1910, Ohio by 1926 and Indiana by 1929, and were nearly gone from several other states. In Wisconsin, there were only 25 breeding pairs left in 1936.

Thanks to hunting prohibitions and the restoration, protection and management of wetlands, they are not endangered anymore; in fact, they seem to be thriving. The US Fish and Wildlife Service tallied about 30,000 birds in 1994. They have returned as breeding birds to Illinois (1979), southeastern Minnesota (mid-1980s), Ohio (1988) and Iowa (1992).

Their fate is tied to the fate of the wetlands.

long, low single notes. It's completely mesmerizing and not transcribable.

The single most prized crane-counting experience is to see a mating dance, in which two birds jump into the air with their wings spread and their long legs straight out ahead of them, then come down and bow to each other, bobbing their heads, before jumping up again.

"In recent years some people have been lucky enough to see a pair dance on Crane Counting day," Bibby said. "But more often, it'⁻ people who live near wetlands, or near wetlands and cornfiel^d get to see this."

The International Crane Foundation (ICF) started t

in the early 1970s to monitor a woefully diminished population of sandhill cranes. ICF is an international research institution in Baraboo, Wis., that is at the center of research and breeding programs for cranes all over the world. The Baraboo facility houses all 15 species of cranes, with many they carry on breeding programs, some of which recruit greater sandhill cranes to serve as surrogate parents to captive-bred chicks.

"This year (1999) is our 25th Crane Count," said Korie Harder, ICF program coordinator. "We've seen a definite increase in the last 25 years, mostly due to hunting regulations and protection of the birds, and because wetlands are coming back on a lot of the smaller rivers. Sandhill cranes need open, shallow water."

Most people don't get out into the river bottoms at all, let alone before dawn to see the mist rising, and trees, hummocks and islands emerge from the fog, while owls move from tree to tree and the spring peepers wake up. It's an eye-opening and ear-opening experience, and a reminder that wetlands are very old communities, of which sandhill cranes are just one charismatic part.

Red-winged blackbirds

Birds of a feather flock together,
and so do pigs and swine.
Rats and mice will have their
choice, and so do I have mine.

— nursery rhyme

Blackbirds of a Feather Flock Together

By Pamela Eyden

Some birds flock together all the time, others just part of the time. Consider the blackbird. This bird lives a double life. In summer, it's fiercely territorial, eats only meat (if you can call bugs meat), lives in nuclear families and fends off intruders with a ferocity equal to a backwoods Idaho isolationist.

When the young fly away in late summer, the blackbird undergoes a radical change of personality and lifestyle. It abandons all interest in meat, mate and private property. It stops hunting for drag-

Red-winged blackbird

onflies, midges, beetles, mayflies, caddisflies, mosquitoes and other bugs, and develops a taste for grain and seeds. It becomes extremely sociable, moving about in flocks by day and roosting in clusters at night, packed in together just inches from its flockmates.

Great flocks of blackbirds are one of the startling and awesome sights of the autumn migration season. In late summer you may see a few dozen birds roosting together. By late September you can see flocks of 25,000 to 50,000 birds.

"I've seen them leave the river valley like a tornado in the morning," said Winona birder and biologist Tex Hawkins. "They go out to work the fields, you might say, harvesting seeds and grain, and fueling up for the migration."

"Then in the evening they come down over the bluffs again, great undulating flocks of them. You can hear their wings as they drop into the treetops. Then they filter out into the marsh."

This "flocking up" or "staging" period lasts until the birds take off for winter grounds. The flocking up and migrating phases may overlap, with some birds continuing to join the flock as others move generally southward.

Huge flocks of blackbirds can eat a lot of corn, oats, sorghum, sunflower seeds and other grain — both ripening grain and grain left in the field after harvest. Researchers say the birds seek food within five miles of their roosting areas. If they can't find food, they move southward. They also tend to hit the same areas every year. If a farm or nearby farms suffer losses one year, they are likely to suffer losses the next year.

In the war against blackbirds, farmers use propane exploders, popup scarecrows, electronic noisemakers, helium-filled balloons, radio-controlled model planes, strands of mylar and a variety of other techniques. It's generally psychological warfare — an attempt to startle the birds so they'll move to a quieter field. No one device works by itself; they have to be used in combination. Even then, nothing works all the time. Birds get used to anything, and if the food is attractive enough and alternative sources are few, they'll put up with all kinds of harassment. Another option for farmers is to plant crops that are not attractive to the birds, such as hay or soybeans.

Different birds have different migration strategies. Some travel solo, like shrikes, kingfishers, grebes and wrens. Some move along in loose flocks, like hawks, swifts, blue jays, swallows and warblers.

Some travel in tight formations, like swans and geese. Warblers and other songbirds travel by night. Blackbirds fly by day, in long formations called "extended clusters" — three dimensional flocks that drift across the land like miles-long snakes or rivers of birds.

Such a flock will be made up primarily of red-winged blackbirds, but can also include Brewer's blackbirds, rusty blackbirds and common grackles, as well as an occasional yellow-headed blackbird and starling, which is not even in the blackbird subfamily, *Icteridae*.

Red-winged blackbirds are one of the three most numerous birds in North America (along with European starlings and house sparrows). They nest in cattail marshes, waterways and wet ditches all across the continent, from northern Canada and Alaska to Costa Rica and the Caribbean.

Brewer's blackbirds are about the size of a robin. The male is all black with startling white eyes. The female is brown-gray with dark eyes.

Rusty blackbirds do not nest in the Upper Mississippi River Valley, but migrate through from nesting grounds in northern swamps and bogs throughout Canada, Alaska and northern New England.

Yellow-headed blackbirds nest here, but spend winters farther south, in Mexico. Most leave earlier than their cousins, departing the northern reaches of the Upper Mississippi River Valley by September.

Flock Mind

Blackbirds have a remarkable and renowned ability to fly close together, wheel and turn, bunch up and spread apart, rise and drop as though all had the same thought at the same moment. How do they avoid crashing into each other? How do they know which way everyone else is going to go from one second to the next? Even if they aren't obeying some kind of weird "group mind", their quick responses to complex stimuli are extraordinary.

As complicated as it looks, computer programmers of "artificial life" have been able to imitate this flocking behavior pretty easily. Each individual moves forward based on the position, direction and speed of its neighbors in the flock, following three basic rules:

First, steer to avoid crowding immediate neighbors.

Second, steer toward the average heading of immediate neighbors.

Third, steer to move toward the average position of neighbors.

Chris Reynolds, a programmer who first created artificial life animations of flocking behavior, called them "boids."

Flocking may offer several advantages: greater accuracy in navigating to wintering grounds, ease of finding new sources of food, and a better chance of avoiding predators. Even in summer, blackbirds will cooperate to mob a crow or chase a hawk. Big flocks present even more intimidating prospects for would-be attackers.

Blackbirds don't all leave at once. In fact, some may stick around for quite a while.

"Blackbirds are short-distance migrators. They go only as far as they have to go to get to fields that are free of snow," said Melinda Knutson, wildlife biologist with the U.S. Geological Survey in La Crosse, Wis. "We don't know if they use the Mississippi River as a visual guide. We'd like to find out. But the whole Midwest is a virtual smorgasbord of grains in the fall, so they may just go from one [source of food] to another."

Some blackbirds, grackles and starlings may be seen in the Upper Mississippi River Valley nearly all winter. The 2002 Christmas Bird Count showed:

- Hastings, Minn.: 0 red-winged blackbirds; 0 grackles; 2,188 starlings.
- La Crosse, Wis.: 180 red-winged blackbirds; 0 grackles; 1,696 starlings;
- Davenport, Iowa: 2,700 red-winged blackbirds; 710 grackles; 5,308 starlings.

Great numbers of red-winged blackbirds and cowbirds often stay all winter near the Quad Cities. There may be thousands or tens of thousands, depending on the severity of the winter, what food is available and how much cattail and other cover is available, according to Kelly McCay, senior scientist at the Niabi Zoo Conservation Science Center in Moline, Ill.

The birds roost communally in the few pockets of wetlands that remain of the historically vast tracts of wetlands that once surrounded the convergence of the Rock and Mississippi rivers.

"These birds established their migration routes thousands of years ago. They might hopscotch through grain fields in the fall, but they still roost communally in the wetlands at night," McCay said. "They leave in the morning and return at 4 in the afternoon; you can set your clock by them."

Most of the continent's blackbirds winter in the southern states, with the greatest concentration in the Lower Mississippi River Valley. There, the great flocks are made of resident red-wings and migrants, along with other species of blackbirds, and grackles, cowbirds, starlings and even robins. This grand congregation of birds roosts communally — males and females separately — in flocks that may contain several million birds!

As awesome as this is, the passenger pigeon was even more inclined to flock together. This now-extinct bird used to gather in roosts that were estimated to contain billions of birds.

A Crazy Heron with a Tackle Box

By Pamela Eyden

There are three herons on the Upper Mississippi. The great blue heron is the most common. The smaller black-crowned night heron is a rarer sight. The third one — the green heron — is not at all rare, but it's the smallest and harder to see. There's a good reason to watch for this small wader: It's a resourceful angler — using live bait and fashioning its own lures.

The green heron is about 18 inches long, with a short tail, short legs and a fairly short, russet-colored neck. Because of its short legs and neck, you may not recognize it as a heron, although, like the great blue, it usually flies with its head pulled in and its feet trailing. If you see one standing on a snag, you will notice the bird's orange legs and big feet. In the sunlight, its deep green back feathers have a coppery, iridescent sheen. When alert or startled, a crest of dark feathers stands erect on the back of its neck. With bright yellow, wide-awake-and-ready eyes, the green heron is a handsome bird.

You'll find green herons by scanning the shore of quiet bays and inlets, and the edge of marshes and small tributaries along the river. Look closely at low-lying snags and stumps, and at the edge of tall grasses in the marsh.

Big River Magazine, May-June 2009

"It's easy to see the great blue herons. It takes a finer-tuned observer to see these smaller herons," said Carrol Henderson of the Minnesota Department of Natural Resource's nongame wildlife program.

Green herons hunt in some of the same places that great blue herons and egrets do, but they won't stick around if these bigger birds show up.

Their favorite diet is fish and frogs, but they'll take insects and other invertebrates. They hunt mostly at twilight and dawn. Green herons are often seen with their necks pulled in, moving very, very slowly, with the unhurried, deliberate gait of a tai chi master, keen eyes trained on the water, scanning for prey. Some sources report that they'll stand with one foot poised in the air for as long as 30 seconds. When ready to strike, they dart their heads out and down, lightning fast, catching minnows in open beaks.

They use other fishing techniques, as well. Fred Lesher, who does a lot of birding and leads tours for the Coulee Region Audubon Society in La Crosse, Wis., has seen them stand on one leg and stir the water with the other foot, agitating the surface to scare up bugs and, perhaps, frogs.

"They also have a tendency to dash about sometimes," said Lesher. "I've watched them run around in the shallows, chasing minnows back and forth — that seems like a losing proposition to me. They have a crazed look, with those yellow eyes and their crest flashing up. Sometimes two birds do that together. They look really crazy."

Lesher has never seen green herons use bait to catch fish, but many incidents have been reported in scientific literature. One of the most prominent accounts came from Japan, although they have come from North America, too. The *Birds of North America* (No. 129, 1994) reports that green herons may drop all kinds of things on the water to lure fish to the surface — crusts of bread, mayflies, berries, leaves, feathers and pieces of plastic foam.

One observer watched a green heron dig earthworms out of the mud and use them as bait.

Even more fascinating is the account of a green heron capturing a live mayfly and placing it in the water. It watched the mayfly for several seconds. When nothing came to the surface, it retrieved the still-living insect and put it down a few feet away. Observers watched as the green heron repeated this maneuver for 30 minutes

Green heron

before abandoning the fishing spot and flying away.

Tool use among birds is interesting and rare enough to get a lot of attention when it occurs. Scientists have studied hungry Egyptian vultures using rocks to break open thick-shelled ostrich eggs, crows in Japan dropping hard-shelled nuts onto the street where cars drive over them and break the shells, and the satin bowerbird of eastern Australia holding fibrous material in its beak to paint its bower. Closer to home, brown-headed nuthatches use bark to pry up other bark to search for food. The double-crested cormorant may use one of its feathers to apply oil to its other feathers. Gulls and crows drop clams and turtles onto hard surfaces to crack them open.

Green herons have another distinction over these tool-using birds. Not only do they use bait, they sometimes make their own, breaking big, unwieldy sticks into smaller pieces before dropping them in the water.

Very few birds manufacture their own tools. Among this rarified category are woodpecker finches, one of the finches Darwin studied in the Galapagos, which use twigs to dig grubs out of tree bark; and crows on the South Pacific island of New Caledonia, which fashion sticks into hook shapes, to dig into loose bark and find insects.

"Green herons have incredible fishing techniques," said Henderson. "People were flabbergasted, when they discovered what they were doing."

While on the river this summer, keep a sharp lookout for this fascinating heron and its tool-using behavior. They're fun to watch and, if you are an angler, you might just learn a new trick.

Peregrine falcon

Bluffland Birds

Scrappy Eagles on a Blue Water Day...33

Peregrines Return...37

A Good Year for Falcons 39

Back to the Bluffs...43

Turkey Vultures — Beautiful, from a Distance........................47

Living with a Vulture..51

Bald eagle

Scrappy Eagles on a Blue Water Day

By Sally Sloan

M arch 21, 1999, was one of the days my husband, Bob, and I
have come to call "Blue Water Days" on the Mississippi.
Blue sky, a few tiny puffy white clouds, the water appears
dark blue, the distant hills look purple and the scene is so incredibly
beautiful that it makes you want to cry or pray. The leaves have
begun to bud on the trees, giving everything a soft fuzzy look. The
ice is almost entirely gone, just a plug left at the mouth of our little
bay.

The eagles are back in force! We have a nesting pair — we call
them Ozzie and Harriet — less than a mile away from our home.
They come to our little bay nearly every day to fish. This morning we
watched as the female (females are a third bigger so you can tell at a
distance) got thoroughly wet and had to flap mightily to pull herself
out of the river after trying to catch a fish. She was sitting on a root
above the water, her mate in a tree on the other side of the bay
entrance.

Everything looked quiet and serene, a picture we see daily. Then
the young eagles arrived. Some are starting to show white feathers,
so they must be about three years old, but others are still entirely

Big River Magazine, May 1999

mottled and dark, so must be only two or so. The youngsters made a few low, hazing passes at the mature eagles. Soon more and more young eagles appeared.

The hunt for fish became intense. A small, young one caught something in the river and appeared to be in trouble, sinking deeper and flapping wildly while dragging the fish (or being dragged) through the water. It moved on and another young one immediately flew down to capture the dropped fish. So it went through several eagles, until finally one was strong enough to drag what turned out to be a very large fish over to the ice plug, where it simply sat on it.

And now the fun really began. Harriet left her low perch and threatened the youngster as other eagles gathered around and hazed as well. The mature female finally scared off the youngster, and then stood on the fish. In moments there were more than fifteen eagles hopping around or standing and making threatening motions. The large female managed to eat. Her mate came over and simply stood by, standing close to youngsters who were threatening, as if to say "Leave her alone. She has a nest." We watched as the female ate a fair amount before conceding the fish to a very large, aggressive young eagle.

The youngsters really got excited by that and started behaving like a bunch of preteens playing sand-lot soccer. They threatened each other and grabbed for the fish and leapt about in an amazing way. Finally one of the youngsters managed to grab the fish and fly off — with a dozen huge eagles chasing. It flew over the water and dropped the fish, which was promptly picked up by another. They flew faster than we normally see, around and around a little island, sometimes trying to get back to the ice patch where it had all started and sometimes aiming at a tree limb. The eagle carrying the fish tried for a tree, was bumped by another and we could see the fish fly in a long arc back into the water. Other eagles managed to grab the fish and fly off with it. Cars stopped all along the highway to watch this pack of rowdy eagles.

Ozzie and Harriet settled down on their favorite fishing perches at opposite sides of the bay mouth. The young eagles stayed a while, fighting with each other, but eventually left. It is again the image of serenity with Ozzie and Harriet perched in a stately manner on either side of the bay. As we sit here enjoying this magnificent show, we feel so blessed to be able to look out from our home and enjoy the ever-changing spectacle of the magnificent Mississippi.

Bald eagles

Peregrine falcon

Peregrines Return

By Pamela Eyden

Peregrine falcons have patrolled the Upper Mississippi River Valley for thousands of years. Fast, bold hunters who nest on cliffs, these aerodynamic raptors can dive at speeds greater than 100 miles per hour.

The Native Americans who lived along the river in Iowa, Wisconsin and Minnesota must have admired these birds. They carved falcon-shaped petroglyphs into cave walls. They built falcon-shaped mounds on the bluff tops. Several of these mounds remain at Effigy Mounds National Monument, near Marquette, Iowa.

Experts estimate there never were many more than 20 pairs on the upper river. In the 1950s and 60s, peregrines here and across the continent were nearly wiped out by the pesticide DDT. The last wild one was seen on a cliff near Effigy Mounds National Monument in 1964.

After successfully breeding captive peregrines and releasing dozens of birds at nesting boxes on power plant smokestacks for 20 years, Bob Anderson, director of the Raptor Resource Project (RRP), wanted to try getting the birds back on the bluffs where they belong. Not everyone thought it was possible. Adult peregrines are fierce hunters, but the young are prey for great horned owls and raccoons.

In the summer of 1998, Anderson and other RRP volunteers rapelled down a cliff to a nesting box, or "hack box," attached to a

Big River Magazine, June 2000

cliff at Effigy Mounds National Monument and set young birds into a protective new home. Volunteers returned every day to feed them dead quail and monitor their progress, staying hidden behind a special blind to prevent the young birds from imprinting on humans. This labor of love took about five hours a day: a one-hour drive to the site; a one-hour hike to the cliff; one hour watching the birds; and another two hours to get out and go home. They watched nervously for signs of owls or raccoons near the box.

All nine of young birds survived the early rigors of learning to fly and hunt on the cliff. A year later one young male was found dead at the foot of a cliff in La Crosse, Wis., most likely struck by a car. This year one of the birds released in 1998 built a nest at Queen's Bluff in Blufflands (now Great River Bluff) State Park, about 10 miles downstream from Winona, Minn.

In May, Anderson surveyed all the bluffs from the Twin Cities to Marquette, Iowa, at an altitude of 500 feet from a helicopter provided by Dairyland Power Company. He rated each cliff as a potential peregrine nest site. "We discovered that we're not missing any. Twenty years of hiking around and watching has showed us all the likely spots."

Peregrines may now be nesting on many cliffs along the river, including John Latsch State Park (10 miles north of Winona, Minn.); Lansing, Iowa; and Alma, Cassville and Maiden Rock, Wis. "Last year we had no nesting on the cliffs. This year we have five!" Anderson said.

Anderson hopes to visit the Queen's Bluff nest one day to find newly hatched young. Then, in his words, "The peregrine will be back on the Mississippi, for sure, forever!"

But is it the same Mississippi? The river has changed in countless ways since the early 1960s. The water is less polluted, but islands and forests have diminished. Many migratory songbirds, a seasonal food source for peregrines, are in decline, but pigeons, an easy prey, are more plentiful. Raccoons, a predator of eggs and nestlings, are also more plentiful; they're not trapped as heavily as they were in the 50s and 60s, when pelts were worth $50.

Researchers are testing for increased levels of heavy metals in peregrine habitat, especially near power plants. One very important thing has not changed a bit: the craggy, steep dolomite and sandstone cliffs that peregrines nest on.

Humans who live in the valley, too, are glad to see the return of this amazing bird to the blufflands.

A Good Year for Falcons

By Pamela Eyden

B ob Anderson doesn't enjoy buckling himself into a harness and dropping over the edge of a 500-foot cliff above the Mississippi River. The edge melts into an ocean of space, the ground below looks a lot like water, and the rock wall is sharp and crumbly.

"I'm not an expert at this — in fact, it really scares me. The older I get the harder it gets," he admitted. "But I can't quit now. I do it for the birds."

Anderson, 49, director of the Raptor Resource Project, has ascended and descended the heights dozens of times in the last two decades to place peregrine falcon nesting boxes and eggs, and to band and blood-test young falcons. For most of those years he worked on power-plant smokestacks, buildings or grain elevators.

Peregrines have done well in these human-built homes. The first power-plant nest box was mounted 11 years ago at the Northern States Power Plant in Bayport, Minn., on the St. Croix River. Since then, 169 falcons have fledged from 12 different plants along the Mississippi and St. Croix. A lot of those birds came from the Raptor Resource Project (RRP), an independent, nonprofit organization based in Decorah, Iowa.

On a day in mid-June, Anderson and his assistant Pete Olson prepared to rappel down a cliff near Lansing, Iowa. No one expected

Big River Magazine, September 2000

Peregrine falcon

these falcons to be aggressive, but peregrines sometimes defend their nests fiercely.

"Those talons are sharp as knives," said one volunteer, "but peregrines usually hit you full force with the backs of their talons as they fly by. That's how they kill their prey. It feels like getting hit with a club."

Hence white hard hats are part of the climbers' gear.

Last year the female, referred to as 6/V, and the male, T/M, nested at a nest box at Lansing's Alliant Power Plant. When they returned this spring they found a second nest box high on the wall of an adjacent cliff, placed there by the RRP. The birds tried both and chose the cliff home.

Anderson was elated. It marked the first time that peregrines shifted from a power plant to a cliff, a goal he's been working toward for many years. The purpose of the June 15 expedition was to rappel down the rock face, retrieve the young falcons from the nest box, carry them to a mobile lab in a truck at the bottom of the cliff, band them and take blood samples, then return them safely to the nest box — with minimal disturbance to the adults.

First the rappellers lined up precisely above the nest box, directed by assistants with walkie-talkies below. Then they checked all the gear, twice. Olson, a professional climber who makes a living cleaning windows on tall buildings in Rochester, Minn., frequently volunteers time to the RRP. Pete clipped two portable cages, aptly called Sky Kennels, to his harness and began rappelling down the cliff. Anderson followed, descending more slowly, until he maneuvered into position to remove the birds from the nest box.

Meanwhile, the parents sat on snags and watched, or flew in swift figure-eights, keeping their distance, but keeping an eye on the proceedings. Anderson reached into the nest box and transferred the young, gingerly, one at a time, to the Sky Kennels.

Safely descended, Olson and Anderson emerged from the underbrush with four healthy peregrines. In a portable lab in the back of a pickup, Anderson and volunteer assistants Dave Kester and Amy Ries attached numbered bands to the falcons' legs and took blood samples. The blood is tested for methyl mercury, selenium, chromium, nickel arsenic and other heavy metals, part of a study paid for by the power industry. Preliminary results show high levels of mercury in Arctic peregrines, but nothing unusual in Mississippi birds.

Big-eyed, snaggle-beaked, improbably downy, with enormous feet that foreshadow their eventual size and power, the birds took the procedure calmly. They seemed more curious than anything else.

The task was exhausting, especially on a hot, humid day, and it was only half over. To finish they had to drive to the top of the cliff, rappel down again and put the birds back.

"It's taken hundreds of thousands of dollars, and thousands of hours to return the peregrines to the Mississippi cliffs," Anderson said later. Many organizations have participated, and many people share his excitement at this year's success. But Anderson has special reason to smile. Many people believed peregrines were unlikely to re-establish their place on the cliffs, for several reasons — great horned owls being one. Great horned owls are one of the few predators of young peregrines. But the Lansing peregrines' nest-box is in direct sight of a great horned owl's nest on an adjacent cliff.

"They coexisted for eons," Anderson said.

In late July, Anderson declared 2000 a good year for falcons. Eleven pairs fledged 31 young from power plants. Three of the Lansing birds still hang around the cliff; the fourth got caught in a stack building and died. A pair at Queens' Bluff south of Winona, Minn., successfully fledged one young male. Falcons were observed at eight cliffs in the Upper Mississippi Valley; three pairs fledged young ones and a new pair nesting just north of Alma, Wis., may also have young.

The birds will begin their migration in October. Many wild birds apparently head for South America. They usually fly fast during migration, taking a week or less to cross the U.S. One bird from Alma was spotted on an oil platform in the Gulf of Mexico last winter. Another bird that was released in Rochester, New York, and has nested for two years in Omaha, Nebraska, was found in Lima, Peru. City-dwelling peregrines may not migrate, if they can find enough food during the winter.

Back to the Bluffs

By Fran Howard

Peregrine falcons, top predators of the skies, continue to reclaim ancient nesting sites in three states on the Mississippi River bluffs.
Nest sites stretch from Lynxville, Wis., to Maiden Rock, Wis. Bob Anderson, head of the Raptor Resource Project in Bluffton, Iowa, said eight of last year's nine productive cliff nests supported nesting pairs again this year. He sees potential for at least two new nest sites along the corridor next year — one pair of peregrines has been seen at a cliff near Homer, Minn., and another near Lock and Dam 9 at Lynxville. That's big news for both the species and the river valley.

Before widespread use of the pesticide DDT wiped out the species in the eastern United States in the 1950s and early 60s, peregrine falcons raised their young in nests, called eyries, high on the ledges of bluffs overlooking the Mississippi River. A captive breeding program, which Anderson began in 1971, helped establish a nesting population on power-plant smokestacks. The first successful smokestack nest was occupied in 1989 in Bayport, Minn., on the St. Croix River. Since then, 14 smokestack nests, stretching from Cohasset, Minn., to Cassville, Wis., have fledged more than 500 young. By 2000, smokestack peregrines had begun to successfully reclaim the river bluffs. Since then, 81 peregrines have fledged from the bluffs.

Last year, peregrines established three new eyries: at Minnesota's

Big River Magazine, July-August 2006

Great Spirit Bluff, just outside La Crescent, on privately owned land protected by a Minnesota Land Trust conservation easement; Iowa's Waukon Junction eyrie in Allamakee County, the state's first cliff nesting in more than 40 years; and Wisconsin's West Bluff in Pepin County.

Nesting pairs returned to six other cliffs last year. The two in Minnesota — Queen's Bluff and John A. Latsch State Park — are both owned by the Minnesota Department of Natural Resources. The others are in Wisconsin: Lynxville cliff in Crawford County; Castle Rock Cliff in Trempealeau County; Maassen's Bluff in Buffalo County; and Maiden Rock in Pierce County. In Wisconsin, all of the cliffs occupied by falcons are privately owned, except Maiden Rock, the last cliff in Wisconsin to report nesting falcons in the 1950s. The West Wisconsin Land Trust recently purchased this bluff.

"Maiden Rock is the matriarch of the cliffs," said Anderson. "It overlooks Lake Pepin and is a wonderful place to watch falcons."

Three sites are ideal for falcon watching. A wayside rest is conveniently located below Maiden Rock.

"If you turn off your car, you can sit in the parking lot and hear the falcons talking to each other, courting each other," Anderson notes. The Lynxville nest is also located by a wayside rest, but perhaps the best place to watch the birds is Waukon Junction.

"There's no traffic," Anderson said. "It is so quiet."

The best opportunity for peregrine watching is when the birds first return from South America in early February until they lay their eggs in April. During this time, the birds are courting and protecting their nest sites from other large raptors migrating up the river.

"Any time a hawk or eagle ventures near the nest site, you can see why peregrines are top dog," explained Anderson. "They come out like kamikaze airplanes and beat up the other birds."

It's also fun to watch falcons when the young fledge in late June or early July. The young falcons taking their first flights tend to stay within a mile or two of the cliff where they were born.

"They are quite vocal when they are begging for food from the adults," said Anderson. "You can hear them from a mile away, if there is no traffic."

In mid-October, the birds begin their long migration to South America.

Anderson estimates that the river bluffs from Red Wing, Minn., to Cassville, Wis., can support between 20 and 24 nesting pairs of peregrines. Besides, there's another population that could also be restored.

"We used to have a tree-nesting population that nested in original growth trees lining the riverbanks," he said. These birds used old eagle, osprey and crow nests. "By the mid-to- late-1800s, we lost the tree-nesting population. I think the time has come to restore the tree-nesting population. If the cliffs become too populated with houses, a tree population would help assure the perpetuity of the river population."

Turkey vulture

Turkey Vultures — Beautiful, from a Distance

By Pamela Eyden

Big dark turkey vultures are often seen soaring over the bluffs and the river, where they are sometimes mistaken for eagles. They soar beautifully, seeming to wheel and glide with barely a twitch of their wings, which span six feet or more. Sometimes they fly together in overlapping circles, as though each had its own way of exploring the rising thermals of hot air.

You might also see them feeding on dead animals at the side of the road, when they leap up in alarm at an approaching car. Their bald red heads look like they're covered with the blood of whatever they've been eating.

No wonder naturalist Julie O'Connor at Hawk Ridge in Duluth, Minn., said, "We spend more time telling people, 'No, they're not really gross!' than anything else about them."

Turkey vultures are the most common vulture in this hemisphere. They range far and wide throughout North and South America, and breed from southern Canada all the way down to Tierra del Fuego. Volunteers at Hawk Ridge count migrating vultures in their annual fall Hawk Count, although they are not technically raptors. In fact, "TVs," as raptor counters refer to them, have been reclassified into the same group as storks. In Duluth their peak migration period is from mid-September to the first week of October.

They favor Louisiana, Florida and the Carolina lowlands during the winter, but some may go as far as Venezuela. Birds that breed here in the Upper Mississippi River Valley and Canada hop over the populations that live in the South. In the winter they sometimes gather in great numbers, as eagles do. The largest roosting site ever recorded is at Florida's Lake Okeechobee, where 4,000 vultures were seen at one time.

They return north early in the spring, like raptors. Breeding pairs arrive in southern Wisconsin from mid to late March, when they immediately begin flying over traditional nest sites and performing aerial displays. They stay in pairs all summer and raise their young.

Sometimes you see them flying low over trees and farmlands, scanning for food. They have a very keen sense of smell, so they can find food even when it is hidden below a dense canopy of trees. In the wild, vultures never eat anything alive; they eat carrion — dead animals. Their genus name, *Cathartes*, means "purifier" in Latin, because they clean up the dead. (Black vultures, a more aggressive species, actually kill animals, but they live south and west of here.)

If vultures see other vultures around a carcass, they may join them, but generally they hunt by themselves. Even around a carcass, they don't eat together. Usually one bird eats while the others stand around and wait their turn.

They eat often, every day, although they can go for several days without food. Their diet is extensive: small mammals (mice), big mammals (deer and cows), chickens, wild birds, snakes, turtles, fish, frogs, shrimp, snails, grasshoppers, crickets and mayflies that have washed onto shore. But, because their claws and beaks cannot tear open thick skin, turkey vultures have to wait until their meal is slightly putrid. This partly accounts for the vulture's reputation as a very smelly bird. Another reason is that in hot weather, they cool off by peeing on their legs (called urohydrosis).

Karla Kinstler once had a close encounter with a vulture. She is director/naturalist of the International Owl Center in Houston, Minn., was a licensed falconer and has a license to keep a great horned owl, Alice, as an educational bird. She also finds help for injured wild birds. When someone in nearby Forestville State Park found a turkey vulture in a ditch one December, they brought it to Karla's kitchen. She called the Raptor Center in St. Paul.

"There was nothing obviously wrong with it, but under stress birds get dehydrated, so I tried to give it fluids," she said. She loaded a small syringe with a slurry of veal baby food, Gatorade and water. "As soon as I picked his head up and tilted it back, it leaned forward and barfed."

The vomit smelled of old dead animals, partially digested. "The smell was horrible. I tried Lysol, Pine-Sol and everything. The smell just got stronger and stronger."

The Raptor Center eventually found that the bird had an old wing fracture that prevented it from migrating.

This bird doesn't need more image problems, but unlike most birds, the turkey vulture cannot call, sing or hoot, because it has no syrinx. All it can do is grunt or hiss.

"They're passive hissers," Kinstler said. "They aren't aggressive birds, but they do have this threat: 'If you don't leave me alone, I'll barf.' They're beautiful when they're soaring, but up close … they're just not what I'm used to."

Vultures and eagles are gliders — they do not flap, they soar. You can tell them apart because turkey vultures typically fly with their wings set in a shallow dihedral, a wide open "V," and tilt back and forth. Bald eagles, on the other hand, do not "V" their wings when they soar. Golden eagles sometimes hold their wings in an upturned dihedral, but they never tilt from side to side.

Many longtime river valley residents agree that there are more turkey vultures here now than 20 or 30 years ago.

"Absolutely, there are more now!" said Ric Zarwell of Lansing, Iowa, longtime birder and a member of the Friends of Pool 9. "As a kid we never saw vultures. Of course, we didn't see bald eagles or pelicans or cormorants, either, in the 1950s and 60s. But now we do. A few weeks ago we saw 53 turkey vultures roosting on Mount Hosmer one evening."

Turkey vulture

Living with a Vulture

By Joan Schnabel

I was never much interested in vultures. Like many people, I regarded them as ugly and kind of disgusting. But last November a friend who rehabilitates birds, Marge Gibson, had a young turkey vulture who needed a home, and I had an empty mew. He had been rescued in Peterson, Minn., when very young, and imprinted on humans, believing that we, rather than other vultures, were his natural flock. Because of this, U.S. Fish and Wildlife (F&WS) regulations prohibited releasing him back into the wild, so Gonzo NVV (non-vomiting vulture) came to live with us.

Vultures are quick to puke when frightened. One can only imagine what vulture puke must be like. No wonder they don't have many predators. We worked hard, using only positive training techniques with Gonzo, and in response he has lived up to the NVV part of his name.

My opinion of vultures changed rapidly. Gonzo was very sociable and curious. Within days he was flying to my fist and daintily taking tidbits from my hand, sticking his beak into the tiny circle created by my thumb and index finger, mimicking an opening in a carcass.

Turkey vultures are only interested in eating dead things. They do not pursue prey. Gonzo eats mostly dead rats, gophers and quails, though he also loves beef heart. His diet has to include bones, fur and meat for him to stay healthy.

Big River Magazine, November-December 2016

True to his species, he did have some annoying habits, like pooping all over his legs and my glove as soon as he landed and being a little bitey. When unhappy he let out a hiss reminiscent of a steam radiator.

Gonzo loves appearing at public programs, but convincing him that the party is over and he has to get back in the crate is difficult. Imagine coaxing an unwilling 5.5 feet of wings to fold up and squeeze through an 18-inch door. At a recent program for an Iowa City bird club, I was holding him on my left hand and reading my notes in my right hand when he began chewing up the notes, much to the amusement of the audience.

I don't think it is appropriate to teach tricks to birds used for education, but Gonzo has picked up a few on his own. He has a spray water bottle that we use to cool him when the weather is hot, but if you take the top off, he sticks his beak in for a drink, raises his head and considers the flavor, as if he were savoring a fine wine. However he refuses to drink from the water dish in his mew.

With the advent of fall we wondered what we needed to do to get him safely through the Iowa winter. The lack of food drives migration, rather than cold, but we weren't sure what would be required for him to live outside. We like him, but he was not going to winter in our house. After consulting with other raptor people, we covered the top of the mew with plywood and wrapped the slatted walls with plastic that we nailed to the posts. Big mistake, because last November temperatures soared and humidity climbed. The mew became a sauna, and we had horrible issues with mold. After making sure the mold was not harmful to birds, we took the plywood and plastic off and wiped the mew down with vinegar. This left us tired, frustrated, smelling like vinegar and vulture, and back at square one.

We finally solved the problem by putting corrugated plexiglas, with spaces for air flow, on the roof and some of the sides. We made removable panels out of insulating foam that we could snap on or off of the slat walls, depending on the weather. At night and very cold or windy days, the panels were on. On warm, sunny days 30 degrees or above, they were off. This improved both the air flow and olfactory ambience in the mew. This plus plenty of food got Gonzo through the winter in fine shape.

It did raise the question of where wild vultures go in the fall, when it gets harder to find food and thermals. Turkey vultures, *Cathartes aura*, Latin for cleansing breeze, have been summer residents of the Midwest for the last 4,500 years, based on bones found in the Raddatz Rock Shelter in the Baraboo Hills of Wisconsin. Although they were once considered rare here, their population has significantly increased in recent decades.

One May morning in 2007, Bruce Ause was on Barn Bluff overlooking the Mississippi River in Red Wing, Minn., when he noticed 20 turkey vultures sunning themselves. One was sporting a blue wing tag marked "45." Research showed that bird had been tagged in Venezuela in December 2006. Since then Hawk Mountain and its partners have tagged 441 vultures in Venezuela, with a total of 55 reported sightings, ranging from Wyoming to Minnesota. They have also put light-weight satellite transmitters on vultures in Saskatchewan, Arizona, California, Minnesota, Pennsylvania and Argentina, collecting a great deal of information about vulture migration. (The F&WS forbids placing metal leg bands on vultures. Remember that they poop on their own legs.)

In Pennsylvania about half the population migrates, heading down to Florida and Georgia. The other half stays put in Pennsylvania for the winter. No one knows why some of these birds migrate and some do not. Turkey vultures farther up the East Coast practice what is called "hopscotch migration," skipping over the birds in the middle to winter in Florida.

The Arizona and California birds, and presumably the other West Coast vultures that migrate, go along the west coast of Mexico and winter there and in Central America. The vultures in Argentina travel up to Bolivia, Brazil and southern Ecuador for their winter. The Midwest stream — "our" vultures — summer and breed from Texas up as far north as Saskatchewan, then in fall head down to Venezuela, a round trip of up to 8,750 miles.

Being very social, vultures travel in flocks. No flapping for these birds, other than to get off the ground. They ride the wind using thermals and slope soaring for their journeys. Northern birds leave at the end of September or early October. By November most of the Iowa, Minnesota and Wisconsin birds are gone as well. As the migration progresses farther south, the flocks merge and become massive. Vultures, as well as many other raptors, avoid migrating over water. The midwest migration funnels over the isthmus at José Cardel, Mexico. The annual count in Cardel averages 1,895,679 turkey vultures. The highest single-day count occurred on October 17, 2003, when 707,798 flew by.

This raises an interesting question. How do that many vultures find enough carrion to eat? They probably can't. Vultures likely eat during the first part of the journey, then fast for the final month or so. Perhaps soaring is as effortless as it looks, allowing them to travel without expending much energy. Vultures arrive in somewhat poor condition at their southern destinations anywhere from late November to early January, after a leisurely migration. Most begin the journey north by the end of March, ready for the cycle to begin anew.

Barred owl

Forest Birds

Haunts of the Red-headed Woodpecker.................................57

Frog Hawks and Chicken Hawks 61

Winter Owls 65

Turning No-Man's-Land into a Nature Preserve 71

Red-headed woodpecker

Haunts of the Red-headed Woodpecker

By Thomas V. Lerczak

I followed no trails as I walked through the mature floodplain forests bordering the Mississippi River in southwestern Illinois. Filtered sunlight gave the woods an almost phosphorescent light- green glow; humidity was low; mosquitoes nearly absent. Ruby-throated hummingbirds fed from the intensely red cardinal flowers. A turkey vulture soared on the rising thermals, high above the towering cottonwoods and silver maples.

Just as it occurred to me that I was within the wildest, most primeval place in the Midwest, a strange grinding, growling commanded my attention. The sound came from two red-headed woodpeckers vying for a hole near the top of a snag, or standing dead tree. For a moment, all seemed right. But then I recalled that according to the U.S. Geological Survey's Breeding Bird Survey, the red-headed woodpecker has declined over the last three decades throughout much of its North American range. I suspected that the decline might have something to do with the changing landscape.

Big River Magazine, January-February 2002

Woodpecker Work

Woodpeckers are experts at climbing trees. They appear much less agile in flight. One of the most unusual behaviors one would expect of a woodpecker is flycatching, or "hawking," for insects. Yet during breeding season red-headed woodpeckers will often pick an insect from the air, sometimes after a convoluted chase. This requires open habitats with widely spaced trees. Indeed, the cavity-nesting red-headed woodpecker is often characterized as a bird of the savannas, a transitional habitat between treeless prairies and closed-canopy forest. But since most of the Midwest's savannas have long been replaced with developed landscapes, breeding red-heads have adapted to other types of open landscapes, such as farm country. I have often observed a red-head flying across open agricultural fields, eventually landing on a wooden utility pole, flying from pole to pole, and hawking for insects over the fields and roads. In some instances, they return after a catch to the original foraging perch. Perhaps the utility poles are surrogates for the scattered standing dead timber in savanna habitats.

Hawking red-heads can also be found along rivers, lakes and wetlands. Floodplain woodlands along the Mississippi River, in particular, appear to provide ideal breeding habitat. Recent floods have giving rise to abundant snags and open spaces.

And, of course, nesting locations must be easy to locate in the open floodplain woodlands, given the many large snags and large living trees with dead limbs. Even logs decaying on the forest floor harbor an abundance of insects. Dead wood, without doubt, is an important feature of living woodlands. In fact, a study conducted in Texas showed that red-headed woodpeckers were absent from wooded sites lacking snags. And given a choice, red-heads may prefer to forage on dead rather than live trees.

Oak snags are particularly valuable because they tend to last longer than other trees. Larger trees last the longest. In addition, the furrowed bark of oaks provides more surface area for insects to hide. And, overwintering red-headed woodpeckers require abundant acorns and nuts, collectively known as mast.

Yet not all oak-hickory woodlands produce abundant mast every year. Many oak trees produce a great number of acorns only about every two to five years. Moreover, the red oaks (black, blackjack, pin, red) require 18 months to produce an acorn, compared with six to eight months for the white oaks (bur, post, white). To complicate the situation, mast years appear to be induced by a variety of unpredictable, interacting factors.

Other woodpeckers, such as the downy and red-bellied, may overwinter in their breeding territories. If mast is not available, though, red-heads will migrate after the breeding season. Year after year, I have noticed that floodplain woodlands along the Mississippi River — which tend to be dominated by silver maple, green ash and cottonwood — support a high density of red-headed woodpeckers in the summer and none during fall and winter. During winter, red-heads may occupy forests that are much less open than their breeding habitats.

It's hard to say when red-headed woodpeckers detect a good mast year. By late fall, they begin one of two major phases of winter behavior. The first involves claiming and defending small territories, one per bird, and storing acorns in snags within their territories. Although oak mast is the most important mast used by red-headed woodpeckers, they also store beechnuts, pecans and even grasshoppers.

After their initial caches are complete, the red-heads enter the second phase: long periods of perching quietly or defending their territories and restoring caches of acorns. The birds apparently move some of their acorns. Even with a strategy of aggressive territorial defense, where a single red-head will drive off any bird that it considers a competitor (for example, blue jay, tufted titmouse, white-breasted nuthatch or red-bellied woodpecker), piracy is common. Sometimes red-headed woodpeckers may even cover their acorn stores with slivers of wood torn from snags. If the slivers are slightly damp, they will form a nice seal upon drying. They may use their beaks to hammer acorns into the deep furrows of oak trees, safe from other marauding birds.

Squeezed Out

I have watched red-headed woodpeckers flying across Illinois farm fields, wings flashing black and white. Windbreaks and circling turkey vultures are often the only other hint of wildness in an otherwise tamed landscape. In recent years, as farm sizes have increased, many owners have removed windbreak trees along former property lines. Intensively row-cropped fields with few trees is poor habitat for red-headed woodpeckers.

In addition, urban areas are sprawling outward at an accelerating pace, often despite only small gains in population. For example, between 1970 and 1990, population gains in the Chicago area were minimal, but suburban sprawl expanded by as much as 65 percent. And where we find low density subdivisions and isolated estates — outposts of future sprawl — we find neatly manicured lawns, trimmed shrubbery and artificial landscaping, with nary a native plant in sight. Would a standing dead tree or rotting log seem appropriate in this picture? "Of course," I would say without hesitation. But most would emphatically answer, "Absolutely not!"

The proliferation of the non-native, cavity-nesting European starling in most habitats across the country is frequently cited as a cause for the decline of many bird species, including the eastern bluebird and red-headed woodpecker. A recent study by Danny J. Ingold, however, concluded that because starlings begin nesting earlier than red-heads, and red-heads are more aggressive at nest hole defense than starlings, they can probably coexist.

For thousands of years in the Midwest, fire was a dominant influence on whether a tract of land grew into a prairie, forest or transitional savanna. The oak savannas and woodlands require fire to exist. The fire-resistant bark of oaks attests to this. Without fire, savannas and open woodlands soon grow a denser understory, where oak seedlings are shaded out. In many remaining old growth oak woodlands, healthy, mast-producing oaks still exist in the canopy, while understory and seedling oaks are scarce, despite abundant acorn crops.

Resource managers use prescribed fires at some locations to reverse this trend, but it is unclear whether these controlled fires will maintain the oak communities. As oak woodlands decline, overwintering red-headed woodpeckers, dependent upon mast crops, may have to migrate elsewhere. Breeding pairs, though, will probably still find a home along the floodplain woodlands of the Mississippi River.

I can still travel to the Mississippi River Valley and forget about humanity within the wilds of the river's many wildlife refuges. But seeing a red-headed woodpecker reminds me of the environmental challenges we face. Perhaps someday, if we rise to the challenge, the bird may suggest a different message.

Frog Hawks and Chicken Hawks

By Pamela Eyden

I love to drive along the river in the summer, especially where the hills come down on one side and the floodplain forest stretches out on the other. It's like parting a great, green sea. The forest seems huge and wild, which gives me hope for lots of turtles, snakes, frogs and other creatures I never see.

The fact that I can drive through it on two- or four-lane highways, though, spoils it for a lot of critters, red-shouldered hawks included.

Red-shouldered hawks — *Buteo lineatus*, one of five subspecies in North America — are among the shyest, most secretive birds of the Mississippi River floodplain. Nicknamed "frog hawks," these birds are agile flyers who live in the forest itself, thriving on a floodplain diet of frogs, toads, crayfish, salamanders, snakes, mice, voles, chipmunks, big beetles and an occasional fish. They hunt from low perches, six to twelve feet above the ground, usually near the edge of streams, sloughs or other natural clearings, but will also sit motionless at the water's edge, like herons, or wait near the entrance of a burrow. When food becomes scarce in the fall, they migrate, but not very far. One study tracked Wisconsin red-shouldered hawks to the tier of states just south of it.

Big River Magazine, July-August 2001

Red-shouldered hawks are so well-adapted to the big, wet, old floodplain forest that they don't mind their nesting trees being surrounded by floodwater. Prolonged flooding, such as during the summer of 1993, is hard on them, though, because it disrupts the habits of so many animals they depend on for food.

For many weeks during May and June, the male hunts while the female incubates the eggs and later guards the young. This strategy works fine when prey is plentiful, but if both parents have to leave the nest to hunt, the undefended young are vulnerable to raccoons, snakes, great horned owls and other predators. If water is still high in June when the young fledge, they risk drowning.

The birds are difficult to study and wary of intruders, so a lot of people don't know about their habits and preferences.

"These birds are very attentive to who's in their territory. You seldom even get a glimpse of them. When you go in one side, they go out the other," said Jon Stravers, who works out of McGregor, Iowa, with the National Audubon Society's Upper Mississippi River Campaign. Stravers has monitored, studied and written about red-shouldered hawks for many years. He wants to learn more about what kind of landscape and other environmental factors the birds need.

In one study between 1983 and 1998, Stravers monitored 49 nesting sites along the Mississippi River from Keokuk, Iowa, to Wabasha, Minn. The average density of nests for this 398-mile stretch was one nest per 9.26 miles. The lowest density was one nest per 30.6 miles, between Muscatine and Keokuk, Iowa. The highest density was one nest per 1.17 river miles, in a seven-mile stretch of Pool 10. Stravers said the area has several distinguishing characteristics:

- First, the forest is made of many different types of trees, not just silver maple.
- Second, there are a lot of frogs and diverse other prey species.
- Third, the hillside forest is continuous with the floodplain. The highway does not follow the river. The shoreline is not developed.

Nesting areas on other tributary rivers also seem to follow this same pattern.

Red-shoulders show a strong tendency to return to the same nest site for many years, but only if their habitat is intact. Otherwise, they may be chased out or replaced by red-tailed hawks.

Red-tailed hawks, once nicknamed "chicken hawks," are the most common hawk in the U.S. They are adaptable to open landscapes that

Red-tailed hawk

humans have altered, which is why we see so many of them and explains their nickname. Some years ago, Stravers studied the competition between the two birds. He looked at nesting sites on the Upper Iowa, Wapsipinicon and Cedar rivers, and found that red-tails were indeed taking over some red-shouldered hawk nest sites. But in every situation, the land had recently been drained, leveed, logged or cleared.

"Red-tailed hawks are bigger and perhaps stronger than red-shouldered hawks. They have bigger feet. They always have the advantage in open areas," Stravers said. "But they don't like it wet. They get nervous and abandon their nests when their nest trees get inundated by floodwater."

Drained wetlands and developed shorelines are a boon to red-tails, while red-shoulders bunch up in the remaining large tracts of unfragmented floodplain forest. Most of these are on public land, where you can't easily drive through and see them.

Winter Owls

By *Joan Schnabel*

Owls come equipped with their own down comforters. Great horned owls generate so much heat that they hatch their owlets in January. Since they do not make their own nests, January is also the perfect time for choosing from among plenty of empty crow and red-tailed hawk nests.

The three most common owls in our area — barred owls, screech owls and great horned owls — do not migrate and remain here year round. Great horneds are the big owls with large yellow eyes and two tuffs of feathers on their heads that look like horns or ears. They are thought to be part of the owl's camo, helping them blend into the bark of the tree. They are also an indicator of the owl's mood — scared: flat on head; happy: mid way; or curious and intent: straight up.

Barred owls, named for the brown horizontal "bars" across the top of their chests, are slightly smaller, lack tufts and have deep brown eyes.

Little screech owls come in red or gray and look a lot like miniature great horneds, but that doesn't prevent the larger owls from considering them a tasty snack. Pretty much anything that moves is considered edible by a great horned owl, including skunks and an occasional cat.

Big River Magazine, January-February 2015

Great horned owl

Screech owl

In the winter, owls may range outside their nesting territory to hunt for food. For owls — as with most birds — food scarcity drives migration, not cold. Saw-whet owls and burrowing owls are true migrators, the entire population leaves its breeding areas. Saw-whets migrate through our area. Six owl species, including long-eared owls, are considered partial migrators, where only the birds at the northern limits of their range need to move south. The rest are considered non migrants.

Owls are well adapted to hunting in winter. Great gray owls can hear prey moving under a foot of snow and can plunge their powerful talons through the snow crust to nab an unsuspecting mouse or vole. Owl toes are covered with feathers for warmth. Owl species that live farther north are thought to have denser feathering on their toes than species that live farther south, and within a species those that reside farther north probably also have extra protection. For owls, longer nights provide more time for hunting. When their food freezes, great horned owls "incubate" it, using their body heat to thaw it.

Screech owls' diets change when the insects they consume in summer disappear. They also change their roosting sites in winter, using tree cavities or nest boxes when it is below freezing, and conifer limbs when it is warmer.

Long-eared owls roost communally in winter. Although they are not common, they can be found here. Long-eared owls are much smaller and more delicate than the great horneds, although their plumage looks much the same.

The extreme cold last year was hard on owls and other birds, because of its effect on the food supply. I care for three non-releasable raptors in my backyard (with the proper permits, of course). I worried when on very cold days last winter Regi, the great horned owl, did not eat. My friend Marge Gibson, from REGI (Raptor Education Group Inc.), explained that wild birds seem to sense when bad weather is coming and eat a lot in the preceding days. Then on very cold days they hunker down and don't expend any energy on hunting.

Regi Owl seemed to do well last winter in the cold, often perching on top of her shelter box rather than inside it. She did not seem at all bothered when moisture froze on her eyelids or the specialized feathers around her beak. But when we got wind chills of 47 degrees below zero, I got worried and brought her in the house. She spent her days in one room, the American kestrel had another room as did the red-tailed hawk. The cats and dog shared the rest of the house with us, and we were very very careful about opening doors, it being hard to remember just who was tethered in which room and who was roaming the hallway. At night the owl and hawk went into their small travel boxes and out in the enclosed porch, because I worried about acclimating them to the heat. Because female kestrels do not winter here, Mollie K spends the whole winter in a large indoor mews with some "free flight" time around the room.

Birds and humans were all happy when it finally warmed up and they could reclaim their normal places and routines.

Some of the more northern owl species, such as great grays, northern hawk owls and snowy owls "irrupt" south when the population of their prey species, such as lemmings, takes a periodic dive. We may see another irruption this winter. While this is exciting news for birders, it's very hard on the owls. These birds are naïve and not accustomed to cars or people, so they always suffer a high mortality rate. Unfortunately our love of owls and desire for the perfect photo can make the situation worse. A great gray owl sighting can provoke humans to the same mobbing behavior seen in crows, stressing both owls and local human residents. A few photographers bait birds by dragging a mouse or a bit of fake fur on a string to get them to fly for their shot. Depleting a struggling bird's energy for a photo raises ethical questions and debates over whether to report the locations of visiting owls.

A better way to spot owls in winter is to follow cawing crows and check out pine trees. Or easier yet, go to the International Festival of Owls, in Houston, Minn., in March, to see a variety of owl species. (Should you get lucky enough to see a long-eared owl this winter, Karla Boehm at the Houston Nature Center would appreciate hearing about it.) Sax-Zim Bog, near Duluth, Minn., holds its Winter Birding Festival in February, where you have a good chance to see some of the more northern species in the wild.

Wear your down.

Red-shouldered hawk

Turning No-Man's-Land into a Nature Preserve

By Pamela Eyden

Richie Swanson is a river-loving writer who has been watching birds and protecting their habitat on a particular stretch of bottomland forest for more than 30 years.

Swanson starts looking for red-shouldered hawks in the Aghaming Park bottomland forests in March, when they establish their territories. These beautiful and reclusive forest birds migrate from central Mexico and often return to the exact nest or stand of trees where they last raised a successful brood. After making sure no great horned owls are nesting nearby, they repair old nests or build new ones to raise the next season's red-shoulders.

On a bright afternoon this spring, Swanson set off walking down a familiar path through the forest. An icy breeze pushed through the bare trees, some of which were showing buds, but snow still covered the marshes and ice crunched underfoot, plunging a hiker into several inches of very cold water. Swanson thought it might be too early for the hawks, but an hour later he caught sight of the bird's round wings and blunt tail wheeling above the bare branches of the trees.

They're back!

But they don't always return. Last year he found no red-shouldered hawk nests. The birds are vulnerable everywhere along their migration route.

This early spring hike starts a new season for the birds and a new one for this seasoned birder as well. Throughout March, April (nesting), May (hatching) and June (fledging), Swanson goes out four to eight hours a day most days of the week. When he gets back to his boathouse, he posts sightings on the E-Bird site online and regularly notifies the U.S. Fish and Wildlife Service.

Swanson is meticulous about his records, which he also keeps for cerulean and prothonotary warblers, rusty blackbirds, barred owls, pileated woodpeckers and many other species that live in Aghaming and are suffering population declines. For several years he did a Breeding Bird Census on three separate sites, and published his work. He wrote bird profiles for *Birder's World*, but stopped when he began writing River Bird Blog, a blog of natural history at Aghaming (still on his website). He's also written two novels and many short stories. "Fiction wild and rebellious, Ecology accurate and unflinching," promises his website.

Swanson is a tireless hiker, but he doesn't have to set foot out his door to keep an eye on the birds. Through the picture window of his boathouse on Latsch Island, he can train his binoculars on birds moving in the tall cottonwoods across the back channel in Aghaming. Mallards sometimes lay eggs in a patch of potted hyssop on his deck. Swallows that hunt from a low-hanging branch nailed to the porch are a steady source of entertainment. Elusive prothonotary warblers have been known to nest in a birdhouse on the same deck.

"When I have prothonotary warblers nesting right outside my door and a pair of red-shouldered hawks across at Aghaming, that is a really good year for me!" Swanson exults. His enthusiasm is catching.

"Have you ever watched warblers feeding five young? They're athletes! Mark Spitz has nothing on them! They zip out to catch bugs, and zip back to the nest, zoom, zoom, zoom!" he said. He went to his computer to check his facts before adding: "I once counted them making 94 trips out and back in 58 minutes."

"I guess I'm more of a scientist than I thought I was."

Hearing the Birds

Swanson grew up outside New York City, and first got interested in birds when he was solo-hiking the Appalachian Trail. At day's end, as darkness closed in, he listened to the songs coming from the forest around him.

"'What the heck is that?' I said when I heard my first ovenbird. 'Teacher-teacher-teacher!' I couldn't believe there was so much music out there. It's so intricate, and I didn't know what anything was."

His career as a birder really began when he moved to a boathouse on Latsch Island, on the Mississippi River, near Winona, Minn., in 1987. It was just a few minutes walk across an old concrete bridge to the area called "Aghaming," an Ojibwe word meaning "across the water." Swanson became enchanted with the floodplain forest and all the warblers and nighthawks, yellow-headed blackbirds, black terns, night herons and ospreys. He felt like he'd found a bird heaven.

One day he came across a red-shouldered hawk sitting on a nest.

"It screamed at me from directly over my head and scolded me with 'kip' calls," Swanson said. "When you get screamed at that loud, you don't easily forget it."

That powerful scolding marked the beginning of a long birding adventure. Just as the red-shouldered hawk was protecting its territory, Swanson set about protecting the woods around it.

Protecting Aghaming

Aghaming Park is an 1,134-acre floodplain forest that was given to the city of Winona in 1915 by grocer-philanthropist John Latsch. It is bordered by the Mississippi River, a railroad dike, the Trempealeau National Wildlife Refuge, an unmaintained road and the Upper Mississippi National Wildlife and Fish Refuge downriver. It was an awkward gift, because it's in Buffalo County, Wis., where Winona police have no jurisdiction.

It was mostly used for fishing and hiking, as Latsch wanted, but new roads were being carved into the park, bringing an increasing number of people who wrecked trees and dumped garbage. It was a wild land in both senses of the word — full of forests, marshes and backwater lakes that boats can't get to, hence full of birds and wildlife, but also an ignored and unmanaged place, where some people did whatever they wanted.

The nest Swanson discovered was high in a tree that was directly above an old power-company road used by off-road vehicles, 75 yards from the park's official access road and 100 yards from an old railroad access road that led deeper into the forest. It was a pretty accessible spot, which made him fear for the birds' nesting success.

Red-shouldered hawks need a lot of forest to themselves. They like to live in floodplain forests, where their diet includes crayfish, turtles, frogs and snakes. They are adept at flying through thick tangles of forest canopy. Their numbers were down in those years, although they've stabilized since, but the bird is still on the Wisconsin list of threatened species, and is a species of special concern in Minnesota.

Finding an active nest was a big deal.

Swanson and other birders from the Winona Bird Club began asking the city to erect signs and barriers to keep vehicles out of the woods and away from the nest, but they were ignored. To build awareness he began leading annual public walks through the area in early spring, to show people what's there and why it is valuable. He participated in a foundation-funded planning process in 1998, which recommended a comprehensive conservation plan to lay the groundwork to protect the area.

A few years later, the old bridge connecting Latsch Island to Aghaming was repaired and then, despite Swanson's and others' protests, it was restored for vehicle traffic. This made it easier for people to get to their boats in a small private marina and to their traditional ice-fishing spots, but with more people came more damage and garbage.

In 2005 the city decided to transform Aghaming into a nature preserve. It hired an engineering company to survey the area and create an "integrated system of environmental, educational, and recreational opportunities" (*Aghaming Park and Trail System Plan*, Barr Engineering, 2005).

Swanson and others questioned the plan's intention to improve an old road and allow vehicles into the floodplain forest. They pushed for a comprehensive conservation plan. The Wisconsin Department of Natural Resources (DNR) disagreed with the city plan's wetland delineation. The city did not adopt the plan.

The restored bridge attracted more people and the damage continued. Swanson formed the Aghaming Conservation Fund and raised $1,400 for a gate to block vehicle access, but the city declined that gift.

In early March 2009, vehicles turned 25 acres of forest floor into a scarred wasteland, with muddy ruts, spurs and damaged trees. Some had gone farther, tearing through 800 acres, disturbing two historic territories of red-shouldered hawk nests.

Swanson called the Wisconsin DNR, who visited the damaged sites and wrote the city a letter explaining its legal responsibility to protect the habitat.

"The city began to understand it lacked the resources and expertise to manage Aghaming on its own," Swanson recalled.

Shortly after that, in 2009, the city contacted Mary Stefanski, district manager of the Winona District of the Upper Mississippi Refuge, to initiate talks about getting help to manage the park. Now, nine years later, the city and the refuge have signed a cooperative management agreement this spring. It's a huge relief for Swanson.

"I'm a nest protector! What can I say?" he grinned.

Stefanski also regards it as an accomplishment.

"We don't get the opportunity to manage properties this large on the river anymore. Aghaming is valuable because it is 1,134 acres of floodplain forest, and that's pretty impressive. It's also contiguous with the Trempealeau Refuge, so it forms a natural corridor for wildlife," she said. "We're just connecting the dots."

The refuge plans no new restrictions on the area. The first order of business is to do a full inventory of the park, which is habitat for a dozen species of concern, besides red-shouldered hawks. There are areas in the park with 60 to 80-year-old silver maples and other trees. The refuge may take on restoration of these areas and try to eliminate invasives, such as Japanese hops and reed canary grass. And it will promote the canoe trail it established there in 2010.

"There will be a lot of discussion about public use of the area," Stefanski said.

Meanwhile, Swanson will continue to hike the floodplain and provide information to the refuge staff. He knows the birds in this forest as well as anyone, and better than most.

"Really, I cover just 700 acres," he said. "I don't know what goes on in the other part."

Tundra swan

Main Channel Birds

American White Pelicans Stage a Comeback............................ 79

Listen for These White Swans' Songs.. 83

Mallards — Adaptable Dabblers, Drakes in Drag.................... 89

Cormorant Wars 93

Looking Just Ducky.. 99

American white pelican

American White Pelicans Stage a Comeback

By Pamela Eyden

You can't help but notice the pelicans — huge white birds flying in big groups that seem to be showing off their synchronized soaring skills. You'll be noticing more of them now, as they gather in September to begin migrating to the Lower Mississippi and the Gulf of Mexico.

American white pelicans are one of the largest birds in North America. Standing five feet tall, they could look many of us right in the eye — although we probably would not want to get that close. The aroma from their fish diet and acidic excrement would be as impressive as their eight-to-ten-foot wingspans.

American white pelicans are even more impressive en masse. A flock of pelicans — called a "squadron," for good reason — often fly with military precision, in evenly spaced lines or long Vs, like swans and geese. Unlike those birds though, pelicans fly with their necks doubled back against their shoulders. A squadron can turn, rise or drop crisply while maintaining its tight formation. They can lock their wings into an open position and soar for long distances with little movement. They are often seen "kettling," spiraling upward on thermals. As they turn at various angles they seem to appear and disappear against the sky, flashing on and off like Morse code. Now you see them, now you don't.

With their big, orange, webbed feet, they are very good swimmers. They use a cooperative fishing strategy in shallow waters. It's worth watching for awhile, for a chance to see this. They swim along together until they come up on some fish, then they circle quietly and move toward the center, beating their wings against the surface of the water. This corrals the fish into a panicked and whirling group, making them easier to scoop up.

The pelicans' most noticeable feature, of course, is the big expandable pouch attached to their bill, which the poet, humorist and birder Dixon Lanier Merritt made famous in 1910:

> "Oh, a wondrous bird is the pelican!
> His bill holds more than his belican.
> He can take in his beak
> Enough food for a week.
> But I'm darned if I know how the helican."

This is not just poetic license. A mature pelican can hold about three gallons in its bill, while its stomach maxes out at a gallon.

After scooping up gallons of water and fish, the bird tips its head back, drains the water, then swallows the fish. To swallow a big one, it may snag the fish with a hook at the tip of its top beak, toss it into the air and swallow it head first. It goes down easier head first. Extra fish stays in the esophagus, not in the pouch.

Pelicans are thought to be genetic cousins to herons and the very odd-looking shoebill stork. There are three species of pelican in North America: the American white, Eastern brown and California brown pelicans. Both species of brown pelicans stay near salt water and don't fish cooperatively. They soar over the water to locate fish, then dive for their dinners. They may dive from heights of 30 to 50 feet and descend as far as six feet underwater. Special air pockets in their bones and under their skin — which are connected to their respiratory system — help cushion the brown pelican's body from the force of impact with the water. The same system in white pelicans makes them especially buoyant. That's why they seem to ride higher in the water than other birds.

Up on the Upper Miss

It's been big news lately that white pelicans are nesting on islands in the Upper Mississippi River, for the first time since the early 1900s. Their traditional nesting grounds are in the prairies of the Dakotas, Montana and western Minnesota, but in the early 1990s small groups of pelicans began to appear on the river, spending the summers fishing and hanging out on sandbars. These were primarily juvenile pelicans and non-mating adults. (You can tell an adult pelican in breeding season by the enlarged lump on its upper bill.)

In succeeding years more pelicans appeared, until by 1999 there were 700, according to Ed Britton, manager of the Savanna District of the Upper Mississippi River Wildlife and Fish Refuge. In 2007, nests were found on Cormorant Island in Pool 13, north of Clinton, Iowa. Those birds produced about 50 young, and all came back the next year to produce 200. In 2009 the colony produced twice that many. The colony split, with some moving off to islands across the river near Thomson, Ill. The population continues to expand.

"The pelicans are rapidly expanding to new islands in lower Pool 13," Britton said. "One reason is that the islands are disappearing due to erosion and getting smaller. They are currently nesting on Cormorant Island [Iowa], Woodruff's Island [Ill.], Gomer's Island [Iowa] and the relatively new Corps-created island, Pelican Island [Ill.]. We typically see all stages of nesting until mid-June. This year, they arrived, nested early and then flood waters came, so those have moved to higher areas.

"We haven't conducted an extensive nest count yet this year," he added, "but there are typically 700 to 800 nests, with 5,000 to 7,000 pelicans in the local area."

The nonprofit Stewards of the Upper Mississippi River Refuge maintains a live webcam trained on the nests on Cormorant Island.

Pelicans nest in large colonies, each pair building a simple nest of sticks on the sand. They are shy of humans, but they don't mind sharing space with other colonial nesting birds. Each has its own niche — pelicans on the ground, cattle egrets in shrubs, great egrets halfway up in the trees, and double-crested cormorants and great blue herons in the treetops. They prefer islands or long peninsulas to keep away from coyotes and other predators. The bird feces kills most or all of the island's vegetation, which denies cover to predators. In recent years, West Nile virus has been taking a toll on young, unfledged pelicans.

Eight to 10 weeks after the young hatch, they can fly. At the end of summer, they join the adults when they migrate to the Gulf of

Mexico for the winter.

The BP Deep Water Horizon oil spill, in 2010, polluted the water, beaches and fish in the Gulf. Long-term effects are still in the making. In 2012 the Minnesota Department of Natural Resources found petroleum compounds in 90 percent of the first batch of eggs to be tested, and the chemical oil dispersant Corexit in 80 percent of the eggs.

Budget cuts didn't allow egg sampling this summer, and samples taken last year are still being analyzed, Britton said.

"We are still analyzing the data from last year's collection of addled pelican eggs to determine what the lab analysis actually means, i.e., are the concentrations of hydrocarbons and/or dispersant at a threshold that we should be concerned? Tentatively, it does not appear the concentrations are extreme but this needs more analysis."

The comeback of the white pelican in the 21st century is largely due to federal protection and the national wildlife refuge system. Four of the largest colonies in the United States are on wildlife refuges. The fact that white pelicans are returning to nest on the Upper Mississippi is a very good sign for the river and for birders.

Listen for These White Swans' Songs

By Molly McGuire

On crisp November nights, listen closely and you may hear the high, quavering *who-oo-who* of migrating tundra swans. Look carefully into the sky for a glimpse of moonlit white birds as they make their annual trip from the Arctic across the prairies and Great Lakes to the Atlantic seaboard. Tundra swans number about 100,000; about 25 to 50 percent stop to rest and feed in a few pools of the Upper Mississippi River.

The Eastern Population of tundra swans nests on the Arctic coast from the North Slope of Alaska, along the northern tundra of the marshy deltas of the Mackenzie and Anderson rivers in the Northwest Territories, and along the Nunavut coast to Hudson Bay, breeding between latitudes of 68° and 72° N.

By early September, before the young cygnets are strong enough for the long flight, the temperatures force them to move south to the northern boreal forest where they stay more than a month. Then they fly through the prairie provinces of Canada, some through eastern Canada, and some through the Dakotas and Minnesota; and on to wintering grounds stretching from New Jersey to South Carolina.

Big River Magazine, November-December 2007

Tundra swan

Their 4,000-mile migration takes about 73 to 84 days, nearly one quarter of the year. It is estimated they spend about 100 hours in the air, flying at speeds of 30 to 37 mph. They can maintain sustained speeds of 50 to 60 mph, and more with a good tail wind.

About halfway through the trip, thousands stop on the Mississippi River between Wabasha, Minn., and Clinton, Iowa, where they rest and feed mainly on aquatic plants — arrowhead, sago pondweed and wildcelery. Many will stay until freeze-up forces them out, usually in December. Researchers believe the swans are in good condition when they arrive here in the fall, and do not need to store up nutrients as they do during spring migration, when they need to have enough energy to start a new brood as soon as they arrive on the breeding grounds. In the fall, weather dictates when they leave the Upper Miss area — there is no real advantage in arriving early at the wintering grounds.

Camping on the Upper Mississippi

Aerial counts by the U.S. Fish and Wildlife Service (FWS) show more and more swans on the Upper Miss during fall migration. In the early 1980s, swans rested mainly in pools 4, 5 and 5a (Red Wing to Winona, Minn.) There was a 700 percent increase from the early 80s to 2002, with the major increase in pools 7 through 9 (Trempealeau to Genoa, Wis.). The November 2006 aerial survey showed a one-day record, 52,000 swans, on the Upper Miss Refuge, 31,000 of which were in the Wisconsin Islands Closed Area in Pool 8 near Brownsville, Minn. Wildlife managers credit good food supplies, thanks to the 2001 Pool 8 drawdown; shelter from restored islands; and less disturbance by people in the Closed Area. After Pool 5 drawdowns in 2005 and 2006, swan use increased in the pool, between Alma, Wis., and Lock and Dam 5 (Whitman Dam). This area includes the Weaver Bottoms, which was one of the hot spots for viewing tundra swans in the early 80s, then declined as vegetation declined.

Researchers found that often swans will rest in hunting Closed Areas during the day, but if there is a lack of food, they will move to the open hunting areas at night. After duck-hunting season, swans sometimes leave the Closed Areas to more productive backwaters, but stay put when there is plenty of food available.

For the first time, the "Management Plan for the Eastern Population of Tundra Swans," by the Ad Hoc Eastern Population Tundra Swan Committee, includes representatives from the Mississippi Flyway, largely because of the numbers of swans staging on the Mississippi. This group determines what size of population to maintain, then how many can be killed by hunters each year. Tundra swans are hunted in six states: Montana, North Dakota, South Dakota, North Carolina, Virginia and New Jersey.

Home on the Road

Tundra swans spend about half their life migrating. Radio collars help researchers determine the route of individual birds, and aerial surveys tell us how many are where at a given time, but a lot of research still needs to be done.

Their numbers seem to be healthy and even growing, but several factors could change this. Tundra swan cygnets take a long time to mature, and must start their trip south before they are fully grown. There is barely time for one clutch of chicks, so if anything happens to all the cygnets, that's it for the year. Swans don't breed until they are two to three years old. Some of their nesting area is near gas and oil exploration, and the development that comes with it. One researcher found that nesting swans are sensitive to human disturbance within 1,600 feet.

That far north, climate change is expected to have a sharp effect. The Swan Research Program is studying trumpeter and tundra swan hybridization, observing that adjacent but separate habitats are blending together, and are likely to cause similar species once isolated to interbreed.

The traditional wintering grounds for the tundra swan was in Chesapeake Bay, Maryland, but since aquatic plants started declining in the 1970s, most swans go farther south to coastal North Carolina. Swans also began flying inland to feed in fields. From 2002 to 2006, an average of 67 percent of eastern swans wintered in North Carolina, many in the Pocosin Wildlife Refuge, where about 25,000 swans spend the winter. Recently, the Navy had its sights on a new landing field close to the refuge, but the outcry from state officials and the public convinced the Navy to look elsewhere.

About 3,500 to 4,000 eastern swans are shot every year during hunting seasons, and many are also killed in subsistence hunting in Alaska and Canada. Lead poisoning is the next most commonly-reported cause of death.

Since the mid-1950s, tundra swans have fed in agricultural fields on their spring migration. Many believe that the aquatic vegetation is not generally available then, and that grain helps them bulk up for nesting and restore body mass lost during the winter. There is also speculation that eating more grain contributes to their increasing numbers, may influence their route and reduces their dependence on wetlands.

Swans take longer on their spring trip, and may be held back by winter conditions. Because the FWS does few aerial bird counts in the spring, it has no accurate count of swans that use the river then. In March 2000, a survey of pools 4 through 11 found almost 23,000 swans. Eighty-two percent of these were in areas that are open to hunting in the fall.

Mallards

Mallards
Adaptable Dabblers, Drakes in Drag

By Pamela Eyden

With their orange webbed feet, brown-streaked feathers (females) and emerald-green heads (males), mallards are the most common and familiar duck on the Mississippi River. This adaptable dabbling duck is actually the single most common duck in the world, and is thought to be the ancestor of all domesticated ducks.

They're so common that many people look right past them. "Nothing out there. Just mallards," say birders scanning for goldeneyes, canvasbacks and other, more exotic waterfowl.

Hunters take a keen interest in mallards, though, especially in the fall, when the birds gather in flocks, preparing to migrate to the Gulf states for the winter. How many mallards there are, and where and when they migrate are all topics of great interest to duck hunters. After all, mallards constitute a large percentage of the birds taken by hunters each year.

The 2001 season looks like a pretty good year for mallards. Estimates of their numbers are down 60 percent from the 2000 estimate, but the 2000 estimate was up 66 percent over the 1999 estimate. This wild swing is due to alternating wet and dry years. This year population estimates are near the long-term average.

Big River Magazine, September-October 2001

Whether hunters in the Upper Mississippi River see many of them is a different matter. Mallards that nest in the Upper Mississippi River Valley tend to follow the river south to their wintering grounds. But most of the birds that migrate through here in the fall are prairie mallards. They come from nesting areas in the "Prairie Pothole" region of the Dakotas and Manitoba. In wet years the prairie mallards tend to migrate straight south, jumping from one watery "pothole" to another, sidestepping the Mississippi River. In dry years they funnel through the Mississippi River valley, where they can find food easily.

The route they pick makes a lot of difference in how many mallards hunters find in the river valley. Ducks Unlimited, the international hunting and conservation organization, has partnered with the U.S. Fish and Wildlife Service and state agencies to launch a major study of mallards in 2001. The research project aims to find out what limits the nesting success of mallards in the Great Lakes area.

More than half of the original 221 million acres of wetlands in the U.S. were destroyed in the last 300 years. Canada estimates at least 39 percent of its wetlands were destroyed. This has a devastating effect on waterfowl. But most past studies of mallards focused on the prairie pothole region, which is so productive biologists call it the "duck factory." Information gathered here shaped the models that are used to guide wetland conservation efforts. The prairie model, however, doesn't seem to predict nesting success or population growth in the Great Lakes region.

Some data show that the Great Lakes mallard population increased from 1961 to 1973, but declined ever since, while the Prairie Pothole group has held its own.

For three years, researchers will monitor 10 sites in various areas of the Great Lakes. They will identify habitats and other factors that affect nesting and reproductive success, such as predators, disturbance and flooding. They will also implant lipstick-sized radios in the abdomens of 600 female ducks to study their nesting efforts, clutch sizes, hatch successes, and the survival of both hens and young.

In 2001 radios were implanted in 60 female mallards in Wisconsin, 59 in Michigan and 57 in Ohio. By mid-July the weekly reports showed mixed success. Some mallard hens had had their first and even second nests destroyed, and were starting over for a third time. Some had wandered off to new areas. Some had fallen prey to foxes, minks or red-tailed hawks. A few had successfully raised a brood on their first nesting attempt.

Whether it happens in July or September, the impulse to "flock up" begins as soon as mallards finish their mating, nesting and family-raising efforts for the season.

September marks the beginning of a new mating cycle for mallards. Both genders go through a complete molt. Males, which have sported brown-streaked plumage since their previous molt and now look exactly like females, emerge with emerald-green heads and bright-banded necks again. They practice displays among themselves for a time before turning their attention to females. Courtship rituals continue throughout the winter, until the birds return to their nesting areas in the spring.

If you're a big mallard fan, you might head to Hanover, Illinois, near Galena, in September, when it hosts its annual Mallard Festival. Home to Whistling Wings, the world's largest mallard hatchery, Hanover calls itself the Mallard Capital of the World.

Double-crested cormorant

Cormorant Wars

By Pamela Eyden

On the Upper Mississippi, double-crested cormorants are most noticeable in the fall, when they migrate from their nesting areas in the Great Lakes basin to their wintering grounds along the Gulf Coast. These large, black, long-necked, hook-beaked water birds are interesting to watch — hundreds crowding the branches of island trees or flying low over the water in long strings. After a few weeks they're gone.

That's why it's hard to understand the rumors of war coming from other parts of the country. Mass slaughters, protests from catfish farmers and a proposed new hunting law are part of a broader picture of anger and antagonism against cormorants that has been growing for two decades.

In April 1999, three guides and seven fishermen in Watertown, New York, pleaded guilty to the slaughter of 2,000 double-crested cormorants on Little Galloo Island in eastern Lake Ontario. The 10 were fined $2,500 each and sentenced to six months probation. Some say they were treated like local heroes after they left the courthouse.

In June 2000, about 500 cormorants and several dozen ring-billed gulls and chicks were shot on a National Wildlife Refuge in Lake Huron's Saginaw Bay, Michigan. No one has yet been apprehended.

On the other side of the law, Rep. Collin Peterson, D-Minn., introduced a bill this summer that would allow states to establish hunting seasons on double-crested cormorants. The bill passed the Resources Committee on September 20, but did not come to vote in the House before the election recess.

Peterson is not afraid to speak plainly about cormorants: "Personally, if the cormorants were wiped out, I would not think that was a bad thing," he said. "I don't know what useful purpose they serve." (Associated Press, 6-8-00)

(Peterson did not return calls from *Big River* regarding his proposed legislation.)

Why the violence and rhetoric? Some anglers and fish farm operators see the cormorant as a direct competitor for valuable fish, and they've become frustrated with the U.S. Fish and Wildlife Service (FWS) for protecting a bird they say is destroying businesses. The FWS points to evidence that cormorants are not responsible for an excessive loss of game fish. Cormorants, they say, are being blamed for a lot of other environmental changes that affect fish populations and "catchability." Nonetheless, the complaints are growing louder.

In November 1999, the FWS published a Notice of Intent to prepare an Environmental Impact Statement (EIS) and national management plan for the double-crested cormorant, which would address many of the concerns. The fact that the House Resources Committee chose not to wait for the EIS and the management plan illustrates its growing impatience.

Delta Buffet

Flamboyant news stories refer to cormorants as "lean, mean fishing machines," and "a menace with voracious appetite." What and how much do they eat?

There are six species of cormorant in North America; all are excellent divers and fishers. The double-crested cormorant is the most common. They mature in four or five years, live 20 to 30 years, and eat about a pound of fish per day, although they'll take twice that if it's available. Biologists call them "opportunistic piscivores," which means they aren't choosey -- they'll eat whatever's plentiful and easy to catch.

In the Upper Mississippi they eat golden shiners, gizzard shad, bass, pike, redhorse and suckers. In Lake Erie, they eat freshwater drum in the spring and young gizzard shad in the fall — the same fish, in the same proportions as those found in trawl catches. They also take young fish released from hatcheries into the Great Lakes. They eat bait fish grown on Minnesota baitfish farms. They eat catfish from catfish farms.

The FWS in conjunction with the U.S. Department of Agriculture estimates that cormorants take from three to seven percent of the annual catfish crop in Mississippi, Louisiana and Arkansas. Some people say the bite is bigger than that. According to one estimate in the *Delta Farm News*, the state of Mississippi hosts about 65,000 cormorants during the winter. Each bird consumes an average of 1.5 pounds of fish, which includes 0.6 pounds of catfish, each day for 120 days. At $.75 per pound, that's a $5.85 million dollar loss in Mississippi alone.

Recognizing the damage cormorants can do to young fish confined in shallow pools, the FWS granted a depredation order to 12 states, allowing fish farm operators to kill cormorants stealing fish. However, this measure hasn't solved the problem and now operators are protesting the expense. One catfish farmer in Arkansas said he hires five full-time workers to drive three trucks and two four-wheelers, shooting 100 cases of shotgun shells a year. On top of that he has to repair the pond dikes and bury the birds.

"Cormorants cost us about 2 of the 6 cents per pound of profit we make -- that's the bottom line," said Carl Jeffers of Top Cat Fishery in Portland, Arkansas (*Delta Farm News*).

From the cormorants' point of view, though, they are just doing what they've always done; it's the landscape that's changed. Before the collapse of the cormorant population, from to DDT and other organic pesticides in the 1960s, cormorants stayed close to the Mississippi River and the Gulf Coast, feeding on native fish. In the last few decades, the forests and backwaters were turned into hundreds of thousands of acres of catfish ponds. The birds still roost in traditional sites, but they fly many miles just to catch dinner in the catfish ponds.

Also, there are a lot more cormorants around than there were a few years ago — in fact, more cormorants in some areas than ever before. Cormorants have rebounded well from their near-extinction. The Great Lakes group has grown by 22 percent or more per year. From a low of 89 breeding pairs, they have grown to 93,000 pairs, according to the House of Representatives' report accompanying the hunting bill. The FWS agrees that the cormorant population is at historic highs because of protection, the banning of DDT and ample food in both summer and winter areas. This has created a number of hot spots in the north.

No cormorants nested on Lake Oneida, in upstate New York, until 1984. By 1997 about 250 pairs nested there. Despite other environmental changes in the lake (the zebra mussel invasion, less algae, etc.), the birds are blamed for destroying the walleye and yellow perch. The Oneida Lake Association wants them removed. "Until the last decade, cormorants have never been a major factor in the lake's food web. Their feeding has caused tremendous damage — not only to the lake's economy, but to our region's economy."

Green Bay, Wisconsin, has become another hot spot. In 1970, concerned volunteers gathered utility poles and got the county to plow an ice road onto the lake so they could set up nesting platforms for the remaining 48 pairs of cormorants. The grader crashed through the ice, but the platforms went up. Today, the area hosts 14,000 nesting pairs of cormorants.

In the Upper Mississippi valley, however, there aren't nearly as many cormorants as there were before DDT. About 2,500 pairs nested in the Upper Mississippi River region before DDT; there are 700 pairs today. In a good year, 3,000 to 4,000 cormorants migrate through the river valley. This is nothing compared to the flocks of 80,000 to 90,000 that "blackened the sky" earlier in the century.

Sport or Revenge

The FWS expects to release its Environmental Impact Statement in February 2001, after several years of research and public meetings. After a period of public comment, the Management Plan will be released. Options include: allowing more depredation permits, training hatchery fish to feed deeper in the water, destroying eggs at specified nesting areas, and harassing cormorants to keep them from nesting or roosting in troubled areas.

"A range of alternatives will be considered in the EIS, one of which will be hunting," notes Steve Lewis, FWS nongame bird coordinator for the Upper Mississippi. "Until we complete that process, we cannot formulate an opinion on the pending legislation."

A hunting solution, as proposed by Rep. Peterson's bill, does not seem plausible. The idea is not even popular among hunters. Dave Otto, a sports columnist in Green Bay, summed it up this way: "Much as I dislike cormorants ... Sport hunting is not the way to go. A lot of people, including this scribbler, feel you should kill only game you will eat. I can't think of anything more distasteful than a bowl of cormorant stew," (*Green Bay Press Gazette-News*, 6-11-00).

"If there is a hunting season, hunters will be killing cormorants because they hate them. That's the wrong reason to hunt. It smacks of the bad old days when bounties were paid on everything from wolves to rattlesnakes."

Cormorants who prowl fish farms will probably be treated differently than cormorants who catch wild fish in open waters. Shooting cormorants just because anglers resent the competition doesn't make sense to a lot of people.

"Even if double-crested cormorants were shown to have a major impact on perch populations, it is doubtful that a control program would be socially acceptable," said an unidentified Michigander in response to a FWS Survey. "It would be like advocating the control of hawk and owl populations so more pheasants are put in the hunter's bag."

Gabe Ranallo, who has fished on the Mississippi River near La Crosse since 1965, echoes this sentiment. "I caught a ten-pound northern in Lake Onalaska the other day, and there was an eight-inch sauger inside it. That northern probably has more impact on other game fish than cormorants do ... Why single out cormorants? Why not shoot pelicans? I haven't heard complaints about pelicans either, but a lousy fisherman is always going to blame something — usually it's the weather, but if he's having a really bad day he might blame the cormorants."

Steve Lewis, FWS nongame bird coordinator for the Upper Mississippi, wonders how much of the cormorant's problems is due to its appearance. "People will tolerate pretty white birds that have poems written about them longer than they'll tolerate an ugly, black bird with a hooked beak and a prehistoric, villainous look."

"Instead of focusing on all the migratory birds that are declining, said Lewis, "I get to spend my time on the one that's doing very well."

Wood duck

Looking Just Ducky

By Pamela Eyden and Reggie McLeod

Nature tends to economize. When it's courting time, male waterfowl sport their brightest, show-offy plumage to go along with their loudest calls and show-offy behavior, which they flaunt to get the attention of females. These showy drakes brighten up springtime on the Upper Mississippi, when much of the riverscape is still dominated by muted browns and grays.

Later in the season — when all chance of mating is over, the young have grown and pairs drift apart to join larger flocks, molting drakes lose their bright feathers and metamorphose to a more camouflaged appearance, similar to the hens.

So when the difference is most important, it is the most obvious, but a measure of anonymity is apparently more useful for community life. (You may pause here to contemplate parallels with human behavior.)

Green-Winged Teal

Green-winged teals don't stay long in the Upper Mississippi River Valley because they're on their way to nesting grounds in northern Minnesota and Canada, but they're vivid while they're here. Drakes sport red heads, emerald eye masks and white epaulettes on their wings during the breeding season, and they sound something like the

Green-winged teal

frogs called spring peepers. After the season is over, they camouflage themselves in speckled brown feathers, much like their mates.

Mallard

Drake mallards continue to wear emerald green heads and high-contrast tuxedo-style plumage until the end of summer, partly because hens continue to mate and raise as many broods as the season allows. Then — just before hunting season — the drakes molt and grow new mottled brown feathers, like the females wear all year.

Northern Shoveler

Northern shoveler drakes change plumage three times during the year. From December through May, they have bright green heads, rufous red flanks and white breasts, and their wings rattle loudly when they take off. Their two other sets of feathers are both paler and duller. They nest in western Canada and northwestern United States, spending winters on the Gulf Coast and Mexico.

Greater scaup

Greater Scaup

As they migrate through the Mississippi River Valley on their way to nest in the northern reaches of Canada and Alaska, greater scaup drakes are bright and bracing to see, but you probably won't hear them unless you're a hen — *Sibley's Guide to Birds* describes their call as a "soft, hollow, bubbling hoot." At the end of breeding season, the drakes lose their stark, high-contrast, black and white look and molt into a streaked brown that's more drab than their mates. Females have bright white cheek patches all year.

Pied-billed Grebe

Pied-billed grebes aren't ducks at all, and they don't really look like ducks. With their long necks and stubby tails, they look more like loons. The drakes spruce up a bit during the mating season, with white rings around their eyes, a dark patch under their chins and a

Canvasback

Canvasbacks

Pied-billed grebe

striking, pale bill with a broad black band. But they compensate for this subtlety with loud calls described as "far-carrying, vibrant, throaty barks." After breeding season, they quiet down and lose these contrasting touches.

Canvasback

The canvasback drake is a striking bird, indeed, in the mating season, with its white coat, black vest and ruddy red head. To attract attention from potential mates, he gives an "eerie hooting goh-WOOO-o-

Mallard

o-o-o, with weird squeaky overtones," according to *Sibley's Guide to Birds*. Vast numbers of canvasbacks traditionally migrate through the Upper Mississippi River Valley to nest in the prairie pothole regions and farther north into Canada.

Wood Ducks

During breeding season, wood duck drakes are one of the most vivid and ornate ducks on the continent. They sport vivid yellow flanks, rufous red breasts, bright white "chin straps" and emerald green manes that sweep down the backs of their necks like Prussian soldiers' helmets. Later in the season they tone down, although they are always readily told apart from their mates. Wood ducks, like their name implies, prefer wooded areas and nest in holes in trees or in special boxes mounted on trees or poles. They nest in the Upper Mississippi.

Nighthawk

Birds Found Everywhere

Crows — Smart and Playful... 107

Nighthawk Twilight.. 111

Cooper's Hawks.. 117

Kestrels — Little Raptors with a Big Attitude 121

Swallows of the Upper Mississippi 125

American crow

Crows —
Smart and Playful

By Joan Schnabel

Take a hike in the winter and you are likely to see or hear crows. They are conspicuous. They will see you as well. And if you show them an act of kindness or an act of aggression, they will remember you and perhaps even tell their kin. Crows are much better at identifying individual humans than we are at identifying individual crows.

What makes them such familiar winter birds? One theory points to their diet. They are omnivores in the truest sense, and because of this they explore a large territory to see what is on the day's menu. Supreme generalists, there is not much that a crow won't try. If you are doing a winter bird count and want to see little birds, you go to a feeder. Those birds stay close to their food. Bald eagles tend to hang out by the river for fish or by commercial farms for chickens. A crow's meal might include an appetizer of garbage, a main course of road kill, a side of leftover corn in the field, and nuts and berries for dessert. One has to range farther to sustain such a varied palate. There is a theory that eating this way requires intelligence.

Perhaps crows also enjoy exploring. How else can a crow find the best snow for sliding, a favorite winter pastime. How else to learn

Big River Magazine, January-February 2014

the best place to cause mischief? How else to locate that great horned owl so you can mob her during the day and protect yourself at night? Crows are intelligent busy birds with more to do than just roosting all day.

Crows belong to the genus *Corvus*, a genus found on all continents except Antarctica. Our local corvid is *Corvus brachyrhynchos*, the American crow. If you go north you can also see the larger common raven, *Corvus corax*. Crows have a wingspan of 39 inches, measure 17.5 inches head to tail and weigh about a pound. They have a distinctive flight, appearing as if they were rowing through the air. Although they can glide, crows are not adept at soaring (gaining altitude without flapping).

In the winter some crows roost in large groups — up to two million birds — with all the attendant noise and poop. There are large roosts in Rochester, Minn., and in Minneapolis by Loring Park. A roost may serve as an information center, where a crow can discover who has a line on a good food source and follow that bird out in the morning. Or it may simply be near a reliable food source. Cities may be warmer than rural areas, and the lights in the cities may help crows see predators and flee from them. And, perhaps crows know that people usually don't shoot firearms inside city limits.

It is nearly impossible to dissuade roosting crows, and success, at best, just gets them to roost elsewhere. Some roosts have been in the same location for over 100 years. Playing crow distress calls, loud noises that sound like fireworks, using specially designed laser lights and hanging effigies of dead crows (not real birds) have all been suggested, with the best results coming from using them in combinations and repeatedly. But perhaps the best advice is to just be patient and wait until March, when the communal roost will disband for the summer.

In the summer, crows disperse to family units. They are monogamous and mate for life. They usually have one brood a year. They generally lay three to nine spotted blue eggs, incubating for 19 days. Young leave the nest at 35 days, but are still fed, taught and guarded by their parents. As with most birds, young corvids suffer a very high mortality rate. Only half of the nests successfully fledge any young, and probably half of the young that are fledged die the first year. Breeding birds, however, have a 93 percent yearly survival. The oldest banded wild American crow (banded in Canada) was 29.5 years old. Corvids, along with raptors, are highly susceptible to West Nile virus.

A breeding pair will often use "helpers," young of previous broods who help at the nest. Young crows get a long learning period, often not breeding until they are four or five years old. Although nests with helpers are not generally more successful, when the helpers themselves begin breeding, they are more successful than birds that didn't serve an internship. Crows remember family members. A relative that has moved to a new territory is welcomed back for a visit.

Most states along the Mississippi allow a 124-day season for hunting crows. Presumably this is for "sport," since no one eats crow, other than metaphorically.

So how smart are crows? According to Kevin McGowan, Cornell Laboratory of Ornithology, crows are "smarter than many undergraduates, but probably not as smart as ravens." Corvid brains are large in relation to their body size.

Crows are capable of social learning, which means they can learn from the experiences of others without having the experience themselves. For example, a cat chases a crow. That crow learns cats are dangerous. Crows who watch this learn that cats are dangerous, too. Later when an "innocent" cat wanders by and crows shout out "danger danger," even crows who have never had or seen an altercation with the cat learn that cats are dangerous. Next time a cat wanders by, those crows will sound the alarm on their own.

There is also evidence, as found by John Marzluff, University of Washington, that young nestling crows learn about dangers by observing their parents sound alarms. Months later, when they are on their own, they know to sound alarms at appropriate moments. This suggests that information can be transferred from one generation to the next. Perhaps choice of the word "twitter" for social media was a more apt description than its originators knew.

We used to consider tool use as a skill unique to humans. Crows not only use tools, New Caledonian crows make them. If a straight stick (or wire in the lab) does not work to get a desired object, crows bend it to form a hook at the end, which enables them to grasp it. Likewise, crows solve more complex problems. For example, a short stick is available to the bird, while a longer stick and a piece of meat are each in a separate box. Crows first try to get the meat with the short stick. When that doesn't work, they use the short stick to get the longer stick out of its box, and then use the longer stick to get the meat.

Ravens have what is called a "theory of mind:" They are capable of seeing a situation from another's point of view. When a raven hides food, if it notices that another raven is watching it will dig up the food and move it, or act like it is digging it up but not move it, because it knows that the raven who sees it bury the food wants to take it.

Crows have an extensive language. Each crow has an individual voice, and speaks in two dialects, a soft intimate one for family members and a loud raucous one for all others. Crows emphasize their messages by lengthening the sequence of caws. According to Marzluff, "corvids are famously loquacious, having extensive vocabularies of calls that convey explicit messages about danger, food, territory, identity, location and emotion." Corvids can learn to "speak" our language, and when they do they are not just mimicking us. When a crow calls the name of the family dog, for instance, it knows that dog will come to the sound of its name, a situation that the crow can perhaps exploit.

Crows like to play. They play tug of war with other crows. They amuse themselves by dropping things on purpose and then flying down to get them. They hang upside down on moss and swing back and forth. They slide down snow banks using jar lids as sleds, then race back up the slope with the lid for another turn.

In *Gifts of the Crow*, Marzluff and Tony Angell explain how young ravens initiate play. The raven who wants to play approaches the bird with the stick assuming a nonthreatening posture and fluffing out its feathers. If the first bird is open to a play date, it lays down and rolls onto its side or back and allows the second bird to beak the object. Then the game begins with pulling, growling, dragging, etc., but after one bird looses its grip on the stick, the other stops and offers the toy for a rematch.

Crows grieve, mourn and seem to have some equivalent of crow funerals. Crows, at least at times, appear to aid injured crows, but have also been know to kill an injured comrade.

So we know crows are smart, have extensive language, make and use tools, have extended families, indulge their young for a long time, have emotions, mourn, play, will try to eat almost anything, have a sense of mischief, pass information between generations, have long memories and have a theory of mind. What hubris led us to think that we alone on this planet have those capabilities? Crows stand ready to show us otherwise. Just spend a little time this winter watching them.

Nighthawk Twilight

By Molly McGuire

Where have all the nighthawks gone? A few years ago their squawk and roar were part of the summer evening soundtrack of midwestern river towns, especially downtown near the river.

The ironically named common nighthawk is neither hawk nor specifically night flying, and now it's not all that common. Many of us remember these dark pointy-winged birds zig-zagging between old downtown buildings, scooping up moths, mosquitoes, mayflies and other insects that fill the warm summer dusk, their cries echoing off the buildings. According to *The Birds of North America* (Cornell Lab of Ornithology), nighthawks exploit water sources, and Mississippi River bugs offer a nice buffet.

Nighthawks will fly high into the sky, and then dive-bomb after insects. Then you hear a loud "BOOM" as air rushes through their wingtips. The males will also make this booming sound to attract a mate or defend territory. You can hear a nasal screech, or "peent," when they are looping around sweeping up food.

The common nighthawk (*Chordeiles minor*), sometimes known as the bull-bat, is in the nightjar family, which also includes whip-poor-wills. The nightjars generally nest on the ground and have short legs and bills and long pointed wings.

Big River Magazine, July-August 2015

Nighthawk

Nesting on flat, gravelly ground or rocky areas in the wild, a nighthawk's nest usually just involves laying a couple camouflaged eggs in an indentation. They also learned to nest on gravel-covered flat downtown rooftops around the country, as natural areas diminished. The rooftop nests have the advantage of being out of the reach of terrestrial predators.

This neotropical migrant flies one of the longest migration routes of any North American bird, from Canada and the United States deep into South America. Flocks of migrating nighthawks are still seen in Duluth, coming down from Canada, and along the migration route along the East Coast. Usually, however, during nesting season, birders report seeing only one or two, or maybe a small group.

Aerial insectivores, especially those with long-distance migrations, have taken a heavy hit. Others in this category are the chimney swift, purple martin and several swallows. The State of the Birds 2014 report classifies nighthawks as common, but in steep decline. A species makes this ominous list if its population has declined at least 50 percent since the mid-1960s, based on breeding-bird surveys and other counts. In Canada, the nighthawk is protected under the Species at Risk act. Data from 1968 to 2005 points to an overall decline of 80 percent. Estimates put its decline in the U.S. at 59 percent.

Counting nighthawks is difficult. Many counts are done during the day, but nighthawks are quiet unless hunting in the air, mainly at dusk and dawn. Their markings make them almost invisible when they roost. They have short, weak legs and actually sit on a branch sideways. It's possible to sit down next to a resting nighthawk on a rock ledge or stone wall and not know it is there. (Once I was alarmed when I saw an eye blink in an odd-looking pile of leaves.) Both males and females will feign an injured wing and try to lure predators away when their nest is threatened.

There are many untested theories to explain their decline. Use and overuse of insecticides in both North and South America may be affecting their health and food supply. Gravel roofs have largely been replaced by plastic-coated ones, which become meltingly hot and offer no camouflage from predation by crows, which have become more populous in urban areas. Efforts to attract nesting nighthawks to roof-top gravel boxes have not shown much success. It will be difficult to restore nighthawk populations without understanding exactly why they are in decline.

Laurence Gillette and Carol Carter reported on a nighthawk survey in 2001 that recorded a steep drop in the seven-county Twin Cities area since the previous survey in 1991. Gillette believes that the numbers were so low that another survey would be difficult.

It's possible, however, that nighthawks that nest in old quarries, mines and construction sites have gone unnoticed. One of the reasons for a dearth of data is the difficulty in taking accurate surveys.

Gretchen Newberry, who studies nighthawks at the University of South Dakota in Vermillion, has designed a survey that will count the birds at dusk and dawn, when they are most active, as opposed to other bird surveys conducted during the day, or at night, like the National Nightjar Survey.

According to Newberry, common nighthawks are abundant only in a patchwork of grasslands that have not been farmed. Numbers may have increased when they started nesting on flat roofs, but she wonders if urban nighthawks stumbled into an ecological trap, as roofing materials changed and became unsuitable for nesting. She does not assume that they will find their way back to natural nesting areas, or if there are enough of these areas to sustain a sizable population.

Although nighthawks prefer open grassy areas, she has seen some sparse nesting on sand bars. They will forage for insects along small tributaries and roost on big cottonwood trees during the day near rivers in riparian areas.

Because nighthawks migrate in huge flocks, Duluth is still a popular place to see a bunch of nighthawks swooping in the sky. Although the numbers now are believed to be far lower than in the past, watchers in late August have seen thousands flying south on their way to South America. Laurence Gillette does not see as many migrating as he used to.

Common nighthawks are endangered in Vermont, New Hampshire and Connecticut; of special concern in Indiana, New Jersey and New York; and on the watch list in Maryland. Gretchen Newberry believes that nighthawks will not be put on the federal endangered list, because the law is written to favor species that are in peril in smaller areas.

A research paper in 2010 studied declines in aerial insectivores and found that birds with long migration routes — such as Canada to South America — showed an acute drop in the mid-1980s, higher than birds that flew to Central America. Researchers theorized that this drop was due mostly to pesticides, including some in Central and South America that are not used in North America. These affect not only the flying insect prey of the nighthawk, but also possibly bird reproduction. They speculate that because long-flyers have more energy demands than their short-distance cousins, they are suffer more when their habitat and food is degraded.

The report cites an earlier study that looks at how common species can decline and still show up on grid-based surveys, making initial declines in a common species much less noticeable than later declines.

Some of us will continue to notice the absence of these twilight dive-bombers.

Cooper's hawk

Cooper's Hawks

By Joan Schnabel

When we think of bird feeders we think of the bounty of seeds and suet we set out for our feathered friends. Cooper's hawks, however, visit bird feeders to feed on birds thoughtfully lured there by humans. If you've ever seen a hawk at your feeder or had your yard suddenly go eerily quiet, you probably had an encounter with a Cooper's hawk.

Cooper's hawks have to eat, just like everyone else. They are stealthy, agile hunters, prowling the forest until they get close to their prey, then putting on a burst of speed to attack. Sometimes they fly fast and low to the ground, then up and over a bush or fence to surprise prey on the other side. With a slim body, slightly rounded wings and a long tail for a rudder, they are extremely agile, built to give chase through brush and woods.

But crashing around in the bushes carries risks. In a study of 300 Cooper's hawk skeletons, 23 percent showed old healed-over fractures in the bones of the chest. In a high-speed chase they are almost oblivious to their surroundings, including humans and sometimes windows. Collisions, especially with windows, are a primary cause of mortality for urban Coopers.

Cooper's hawks, sharp shinned hawks and northern goshawks all belong to the genus *accipiter*, found in the family *Accipitridae* along with other hawks, eagles, kites and harriers. Like many raptors, they exhibit reverse sexual dimorphism, with the females growing larger (11.6 to 24 ounces, 16 to 19 inches long, with a 31-to-34-inch wingspan) than the males (7.8 to 14.5 ounces, 14 to 16 inches long, with a 28-to-30-inch wingspan). Juvenile birds have pale breasts with some brown vertical streaks, brown backs and pale eyes. Adults have more grayish blue on their backs and white breasts with reddish horizontal barring. Their eyes change color over time to orange and then to a deep demonic red that is most pronounced on males.

(Many other birds have red eyes or develop them as they mature — wood ducks, canvasbacks, horned grebes, American bitterns, sandhill cranes, American coots — but no one knows why.)

When you can't identify them by their plumage, you may be able to identify accipiters by their flight pattern — flap-flap-flap, glide, flap-flap-flap, glide, etc, rather than continual flapping or soaring. If you find it difficult to distinguish between the Coops and the similar, but slightly smaller sharp-shins, don't worry, you are not alone.

Cooper's hawks hunt small feeder birds, but also a large number of pigeons, mourning doves and starlings, as well as robins, jays, northern flickers, pheasants, grouse and small raptors. An avian diet is not without risks. Pigeons and doves may transmit trichamonis (frounce), a disease that can be deadly for nestlings. Cooper's also hunt chipmunks, rabbits, mice, squirrels and bats. Poultry is sometimes on the menu. The epithet "chicken hawk," which is used for both Cooper's and red-tailed hawks, refers to diet rather than to lack of bravery.

Unlike falcons, who use their beaks to sever the spine of their prey, Cooper's hawks kill by sinking their talons into their prey, holding it away from their body to prevent possible injury to themselves and squeezing multiple times with their feet. On average, a Coop eats 12 percent of its body weight a day. To eat like a Cooper's hawk, a person weighing 150 pounds would eat 18 pounds of food a day. So telling someone they "eat like a bird" may not be a compliment.

Cooper's hawks breed throughout the U.S. While some are migratory, most stay on the same territory throughout the year. Originally forest birds, they have adapted well to any landscape with a few trees in it — country, urban, suburban — any place can be home. Like other raptors, juvenile birds have a mortality rate of 60 to 70 percent in their first year.

Although population estimates vary widely, the species appears to be doing very well and is considered a species of "least concern." This was not always the case, as their numbers were greatly reduced by DDT and by widespread shooting for the mistaken idea that they eat a lot of chickens. Although the Migratory Bird Treaty was enacted in 1916, hawks were not protected by the treaty until it was amended in 1972.

Cooper's hawks are generally monogamous, often staying with the same mate more than one year. They have one clutch a year. They build a nest of sticks, with a cup-like depression in the middle lined with bark flakes and some greenery. Nests are usually placed about two-thirds of the way up a suitable tree, often a conifer. They may use nests for up to three years or build a new one after a year.

Given that female Cooper's hawks eat middle-sized birds, the smaller male is submissive — perhaps wary — of the female. He waits and listens for a reassuring call before approaching. Females, on average, lay four eggs and are responsible for incubating, which takes from 30 to 36 days.

Covered with white down, the young weigh an ounce (28 grams) when they hatch. The male brings food to his mate and later to the young, although they always transfer food away from the nest and the female does the actual feeding. Young fledge at 30 to 34 days, but are not completely independent until eight weeks old.

Because they are high strung and easily stressed, you will almost never see Cooper's hawks used as education birds at raptor centers or in programs. You will have to go outside, where they are fairly common year around, and easily distinguished from other raptors, except their sharp-shinned cousins. But you may not need to go far — just keep a well-stocked bird feeder close by and they may come to you.

Kestrel

Kestrels — Little Raptors with a Big Attitude

By Joan Schnabel

What's feisty, loud, opinionated and weighs 4.5 ounces? Meet the American kestrel, our smallest falcon. Over the past four years, I have had the pleasure of living with Mollie Kestrel, a survivor of West Nile virus and my partner at environmental education events.

She considers herself a fearsome raptor, in spite of her size. She screams, or "keks," at her vulture neighbor, even though he outweighs her 18 to 1 and has no desire to eat her. She wants the world to know that she disapproves of his very existence.

When Mollie needs her beak trimmed, she screams nonstop — unnerving humans conducting the procedure. Many raptors go silent and passive, but not this little bundle of fury. It must be incredibly hard to keep screaming while someone is working on your beak with an emery board, but she manages to keep it up for the five minutes or so it takes. It's hard to know who is more relieved when it's over, her or us.

You might see two other species of falcons in our area. Merlins, slightly bigger than kestrels, are usually only passing through on

Big River Magazine, September-October 2017

migration. Peregrines, once wiped out of the Upper Midwest by DDT poisoning, now make their homes on cliffs, bridges and tall buildings.

All falcons have pointed, swept-back wings and flap continuously in flight. Falcons have little cones, or tubercles, in their nostrils to help direct the airflow when they dive. Most raptors kill with their feet, but falcons have a "tomial tooth" on their beaks, which they use to sever the spinal cord of their prey. Peregrines and kestrels both have a "malar stripe" on their faces, which looks like a mustache. Interestingly, the avian family tree puts falcons very close to parrots and far from hawks, in terms of evolutionary kinship, making a common name for kestrels — sparrow hawk — even more of a misnomer.

You can often spot kestrels sitting on a wire bobbing their heads and tails. If you see a small bird beating its wings and hovering in the air, chances are that's a kestrel. Even though they look small, their wingspan is about 2 feet. Like most raptors, the females are larger than the males — known as reverse sexual dimorphism — but unlike most raptors, males and females have different plumages. The females have streaking on their fronts and barred brown-black wings, back and tail. The males' wings are a beautiful blue-gray. Their back is a rusty red, and their tail is red with a dark band and white spots at the bottom.

While kestrels eat small birds, mice, voles, bats and snakes, insects such as dragonflies and grasshoppers form a major part of their summer diet. These elegant flyers can snack on the wing — sometimes snatching dragonflies out of the air and eating them like candy. Unlike humans, kestrels can see ultraviolet light, a handy skill for hunting. For instance, vole urine is visible in ultraviolet light, so kestrels can follow a pee trail to an unsuspecting vole.

Kestrels are cavity nesters and will use a small tree cavity or a box that people make for them. The female does most of the incubating over a period of about 30 days. She usually has four to six young in a single hatch. The male does most of the hunting. The young fledge — or leave the nest — at four weeks but stay with the adults for several more weeks to master flying and hunting skills. Although a few over-winter here, most kestrels migrate to the southern U.S. or Central America. Juveniles go first, followed by the females and males. Pairs winter separately. Females winter in more open areas, the males in more wooded ones. Kestrels mate for life and appear to return to the same wintering and nest sites.

Although many raptor species have recovered from 20th century declines, kestrels are not doing as well. While kestrels have not been placed on the endangered species list or classified overall as a species of concern, the magnitude and rapidity of their decline has caused some states to rethink that. The Audubon Society estimates that the kestrel population declined 66 percent in the 44 years from 1966 to 2010. Some areas lost more than others, especially New England and the Atlantic coast at 88 percent.

No one knows why. Perhaps there are many contributing factors. Because they nest in cavities and hunt over open fields, kestrels need both wooded and open habitat. Humans have been destroying both with abandon. They may also face increased competition for tree cavities from starlings, which are not native. West Nile virus may also be a problem but is probably not a major factor, as kestrels' decline began before West Nile spread in the U.S. Cooper's hawks are doing well, and they prey on kestrels. Statistics show that as Cooper's hawk populations go up, the number of kestrels go down.

Climate change may be shifting kestrels out of sync with their food sources. Environmental contaminants such as brominated flame retardants, found in circuit boards and textiles, may play a role. We know that mice poisoned by rodenticides can kill raptors that eat them. And insecticides may be harming kestrels directly by reducing a major food source or indirectly by damaging the health of the birds. These possibilities have not yet been studied.

When Mollie Kestrel and I go out and do programs, I ask the kids in the audience to tell me what DDT is. The adults all know, but with the exception of an occasional nerdy kid, none of the kids do. We have to keep teaching that story to our children and reminding ourselves of it. We need to figure out what is causing this profound decline and work to fix it. It would be a loss to future generations to never hear the indignant "killy-killy-killy" of a little wild female telling you what she thinks of the world we share.

Rough-winged swallow

Chimney swift

Swallows of the Upper Mississippi

By Thomas V. Lerczak

The late July heat dissipated slowly as the sun approached the horizon. The air above the Mississippi River was filled with swallows. All six species common to the Midwest were foraging on the wing for flying insects. It was an impressive display of life.

A basic principle of ecology states that no more than one species can fill exactly the same role, or niche, in an ecosystem. Yet here were six aerial insectivores apparently all feeding in the same way, in the same place, on the same food. This July scene, however, illustrated only the portion of their lives where the most competition occurs. Earlier in the year, after the swallows arrive on the breeding grounds from distant overwintering areas, the behavior of each species begins to diverge so that all may coexist and produce a new generation for the future.

Rough-winged and Bank Swallows

Rough-winged and bank swallows nest in burrows in vertical soil exposures, such as high stream banks. Rough-wings also nest in other types of holes and crevices. Bank swallows excavate their own burrows several feet into the soil and form small to large colonies. It is

Big River Magazine, August 1999

not certain whether rough-winged swallows excavate their own burrows or simply use abandoned burrows of belted kingfishers or bank swallows. Although the rough-wings are the most solitary of the Midwestern swallows, sometimes they nest on the edge of a bank swallow colony. We might expect the more numerous bank swallows to drive out the rough-wings, but both species seem to tolerate each other. Because predators are less likely to attack nests near the edge of the colony, perhaps bank swallows benefit, but how do the rough-wings benefit?

There are many disadvantages of nesting in large colonies. One study in Michigan by John L. Hoogland and Paul W. Sherman showed that as the colony size increases, competition for nest sites, nest materials and mates increases. Parents are also less likely to recognize their own still-dependent fledglings after the young aggregate into large groups. Parents might then partially raise another pair's young at the expense of their own. Another disadvantage of colonies is that as colony size increases, fleas and swallow bugs (a wood tick-sized, bloodsucking bedbug) are more easily transmitted. So again, why should rough-winged swallows accept all of the disadvantages and locate themselves on the edge of a bank swallow colony?

Even though large colonies have many disadvantages, and they can actually attract the attention of predators, colonies are highly effective at detecting and harassing predators.

Cliff Swallows

Cliff swallows are even more colonial and social than bank swallows. They build gourd-shaped nests of mud attached to cliffs, the undersides of bridges and buildings. Because of this, cliff swallows do not compete with bank and rough-winged swallows for nesting sites. Probably because they nest under bridges, their range is expanding. A very large colony, for example, nests under the US 136 bridge to Keokuk, Iowa, directly over the Mississippi River. Cliff swallows in groups spend less time looking for predators and are more efficient at gathering mud than lone swallows. Breeding is highly synchronized within the colony, and members lead each other to food sources.

The highly social cliff swallows, however, compound the disadvantages of nesting in a colony. A female may not only lay eggs in another cliff swallow's nest, but may first toss out the host's eggs. Infestations of fleas and bugs at cliff swallow colonies can defy the imagination. In an intensive, long-term study in Nebraska, Charles R.

Brown and Mary Bomberger Brown found as many as 2,500 swallow bugs in some nests. Nestlings in highly infected nests did poorly compared with those in cleaner nests. Bug infestations can actually be so bad that cliff swallows may not use a colony site every year, presumably to allow the bugs to die.

Barn Swallows

Although groups of barn swallow nests are referred to as "colonies," the species is much less social than bank and cliff swallows. The birds seem to go about their activities alone, not exhibiting the social qualities of the tightly knit cliff or bank swallow colonies. Barn swallows, as the name implies, build their bowl-shaped nests of mud pellets mainly on artificial structures, such as buildings and bridges. In the past, nesting sites may have been limited to cave entrances and cliffs. So, like the cliff swallow, barn swallows increased with the advance of roads and buildings across the landscape.

Barn swallows tend to forage low over the water or following the contours of the ground. Cliff swallows, in contrast, may fly to considerable heights in close-knit flocks following swarms of insects rising on warm air. This small difference in foraging style may be enough to reduce niche overlap so that both species can co-exist in an area. But actually, cliff swallows are more aggressive than barn swallows and may usurp barn swallow nests.

The barn swallow is the only Midwestern swallow that regularly has two broods in succession. The energy for a long fall migration to South America must be tremendous, a second brood notwithstanding. Some barn swallows I observed nesting in an abandoned boathouse on the Illinois River were very fortunate. The river and its backwaters produce a prodigious number of insects. One evening on the sandy bank of the Illinois River opposite the confluence of the Spoon River, I watched thousands of newly emerged mayflies hovering as much as 10 to 15 feet above the shore, but not very far out over the river. Every once in a while a fast flying swallow plowed through the delicate cloud. That same evening, clouds of midges seemed to dance about over the surface of the river. There are always insects over the river. And the swallows take full advantage.

Tree Swallows

Tree swallows, even more than barn swallows, are attracted to the Mississippi River Valley by the great number of flood-killed trees on the bottomlands. Tree swallows nest in dead trees and snags, in holes and in cavities made by other species, such as woodpeckers. They also use artificial nest boxes. This is a major difference between tree swallows and the bank, cliff, barn and rough-winged swallows — although rough-wings may occasionally use tree holes. Snags tend to be haphazardly spread across the landscape, so tree swallows are solitary nesters. In areas where snags are abundant, such as a beaver pond or a flood-killed bottomland forest, tree swallows attempt to nest as far apart as possible. In fact, a study by Wallace B. Rendell and Raleigh J. Robertson in Canada showed that tree swallows set up and defend territories around nest sites, where each territory may include several suitable nesting cavities.

Competition for cavities also occurs between tree swallows and other species. The aggressive house wren is very abundant in floodplain forests, and probably is a formidable competitor for nesting cavities. Arriving on the breeding grounds as early as possible is one way to win nest sites, but insect-eating birds must wait for warmer weather. Unlike other swallows, however, tree swallows can push their spring arrival earlier by foraging on berries and seeds in addition to flying insects. Tree swallows and rough-winged swallows on average migrate less far than other swallows. Some tree and rough-winged swallows winter along the Gulf of Mexico, while the other swallow species migrate from as far as South America. Even so, aggressive, non-native house sparrows and starlings, around all winter, undoubtedly claim many cavities early in the season.

Purple Martins

The purple martin is the largest Midwestern swallow. Like tree swallows, purple martins used to nest mainly in tree holes or other cavities. Today, though, purple martins in the Midwest build nests mostly in the familiar martin apartment houses. They are probably not naturally a very social species. It is likely that purple martin nests were once scattered over the landscape much like tree swallow nests. Undoubtedly there must have been some competition with tree swallows for cavities, but the martin is much larger and would need bigger cavities. In flight, purple martins regularly soar much more than any of the other species. Watching midsummer flocks of mixed swallows over the Mississippi River, the few purple martins clearly stood out.

Soon after sunrise during the breeding season, the Mississippi

Purple martin

River Valley is saturated with bird songs, including those of numerous swallows. The drive to reproduce must be one of the great forces of nature, a goal of life to be met at all costs. What other force could drive these birds to migrate hundreds or even thousands of miles, set up and defend a territory, choose a mate, build a nest, rear young, return to wintering areas, and then turn around and do it all over again? Why not simply stay in the tropics — single and carefree?

Junco

Seasons of Birding

Waves of Waterfowl 133

Birding in Winter 139

Eavesdrop on the Owls of Winter 147

Birds in January 151

Birds in February 153

Birds in March 157

Birds in April 159

Birds in May 163

Paddling for Birds on the Mississippi 165

Favorite Fall Birding Spots on the Upper Mississippi 171

Dabblers

Waves of Waterfowl

By Pamela Eyden

The fall migration of ducks, geese and swans through the Upper Mississippi River valley is one of the great wonders of the river. More waterfowl migrate to their wintering grounds through the Upper Mississippi than through any other flyway in North America.

"The migration is triggered by the angle of the light and the amount of daylight. Then the pace depends on food supply and weather," said Brian Stemper, wildlife biologist with Upper Mississippi River Wildlife and Fish Refuge. "Wildlife know how much energy they have to expend to get food and what they need to survive."

Ducks, geese and swans don't all come at once, but in waves. Hunters plan accordingly.

First Wave

Wood ducks, and blue-winged and green-winged teal are first on the move, along with some mallards. Duck hunting guides advertise these for their early duck hunts.

But, which comes first — the migration or the duck hunting season?

"At the first of the season, hunters are usually shooting local

Wood ducks

ducks who have lived their whole lives in the area. When hunters start shooting at them, they get up and move south, then hunters south of them say they are migrating," observed birder and duck hunter Mike Kennedy of Winona, Minn.

Wood ducks, teal and other "dabblers" get their food in shallow water, turning their tails up and their bills down to dabble for tubers and other tasty morsels in the mud below. Their small, light bodies are more sensitive to cold than birds that stick around later. When the ponds and shallows are about to freeze over, they move south.

Blue-winged teal migrate farther south than any other North American waterfowl. A blue-wing banded near Oak Lake, Manitoba, was shot by a hunter near Lima, Peru, more than 4,000 miles to the south.

Second Wave

Around about mid-October, another push of dabblers, which are also called puddle ducks, comes through, including northern shovelers, gadwalls, wigeon, and some pintails and black ducks.

Blue-winged teal

Third Wave

Not far behind are the first diving ducks.

"Diving ducks get their food in deeper water. They have larger bodies than dabblers and more feathers for warmth. They tend to aggregate, pooling together in large numbers, which is safer for them since they prefer open stretches of water," said Kennedy.

Ring-necked ducks and canvasbacks are two diving ducks that are common on the refuge. In late October and early November, more than half of the canvasback population in North America gathers on the Upper Mississippi between Minnesota, Wisconsin and Iowa.

Hundreds of thousands of canvasbacks hang out in "voluntary avoidance areas" (closed to hunting) on the refuge, "especially in pools 7, 8, 9 and 13," said Stemper. "We separate these areas so the birds spread out throughout the river. Safe from hunters, they loaf and feed on wild celery and wild rice that's fallen off and gone to the bottom."

Canvasbacks in flight.

They move on when they can't find food so easily or when cold fronts bring wind, snow and ice to the river. Either way, hunger will push them onward.

"Ducks recognize a cold front often before we do," said Stemper. "There are days when ducks just keep moving all day, because of wind and weather."

Northwest winds push the birds along on their migration and signal hunters that new birds are coming in. Southerly winds encourage the birds to stay put.

Severe weather occasionally triggers a mass migration of waterfowl, known as a "grand passage." A famous one in recent times occurred in early November 1995, after a severe blizzard in the Prairie Pothole Region. Moving en masse, as many as 90 million migrating ducks and geese jammed radar systems and grounded flights in Omaha, Neb., and Kansas City, Mo.

Last Wave

Tundra swans arrive from the Arctic at the end of October, with their numbers peaking around Thanksgiving. Resident giant Canada geese migrate earlier than ones from up north, but there's a steady movement all season.

Mallards may migrate throughout the season too, since they get along pretty well in both shallow and deep water. They are often the last to migrate in large numbers, usually not appearing until the second or third week of November. They trail behind the canvasbacks.

Other cold-hardy divers, such as redheads, buffleheads and common mergansers, may stick around until the river freezes up or the food runs out — January sometimes.

Pileated woodpecker

Birding in Winter

By Pamela Eyden

If you feel restless, anxious or claustrophobic this winter, you may be suffering from "nature deficit disorder." Richard Louv, who coined this phrase in his book *Last Child in the Woods*, mourned the lot of children who have lost their connection with the outdoors. But it can be a seasonal problem for adults, too. One preventive measure is to go outside and watch birds. Some flew south to get here, and others just stick around all year, surviving in many amazing ways.

Sit Still

Mike Kennedy, owner of Bird-Song, a birding store in Winona, Minn., goes birding all kinds of ways in the winter, but he talks most enthusiastically of sitting outside and watching them.

"My favorite thing is to go sit in the sun in an out-of-the-way place, maybe behind a screen of bushes, and watch what happens. You have to be quiet for 10 or 15 minutes. That's what most people can't do — five minutes can seem like a lifetime — but do it, and things will start happening. There are a lot of birds out there in the winter.

"Chickadees are very common and they are one of the most fun birds to watch. Did you know they have from 16 to 20 different calls

Big River Magazine, January-February 2011

White-breasted nuthatch

that they use to communicate with each other?

"I like watching nuthatches, too — they make little 'meep-meep' sounds as they climb up and down trees."

Kennedy scans the tree trunks for little brown creepers, also great climbers, and likes blue jays for their bold, brazen calls. "They're so full of hot air!"

If you sit still long enough, even downy woodpeckers might come and sit on your knee, Kennedy said, admitting that it might make a person nervous to have a woodpecker on his leg.

In the Mississippi River backwaters near his family cabin at Weaver, Minn., Kennedy spreads birdseed on flat surfaces, such as fallen trees, in places where he knows birds gather. He skis to many of those backwater spots, but emphasizes that he only skis on the backwaters he knows, and never on the edges of the Main Channel. Springs and streams can create thin ice and hazardous conditions that you can't know about if you are not familiar with an area.

How do you dress for a winter birding trip in the woods and backwaters?

Kennedy likened it to dressing for cross country skiing — dress in layers and carry a down parka and/or a thin Mylar blanket with you in case you decide to sit awhile.

Chickadee

Driving Blind

Pat Fisher, president of the Dubuque, Iowa, Audubon Society, is equally enthusiastic about winter birding, but she has a different approach: She goes birding by car on country roads where there isn't much traffic.

"The car is like a moving bird blind," she explained. "We go slow and use our flashers, and scan for birds at the edges of the road or in the open fields."

She looks for juncoes — the original "snowbirds" — with their slate gray backs and snowy white breasts, and tree sparrows, with their red caps and black spots on their breasts. If farmers have spread manure on their fields, that's where many birds will gather.

Horned larks, snow buntings and rough-legged hawks are seen in the Upper Mississippi River Valley only in winter.

Horned larks, which summer in Canada, are often found in big flocks, flying low to the ground or foraging in cornfields. They get their name from a pair of tiny black feathers that sometimes stand erect on the backs of their heads.

Snow buntings are the rarest winter birds. They breed only in the high Arctic.

Junco

Rough legged hawks migrate into the river valley from the Arctic tundra. This big hawk has feather-covered legs; long, broad wings with a black patch at the wrist; and a wide black band across its tail. Look for them perching on low stumps, scanning open areas for a lunch of mice, voles or birds.

Fisher also has good luck birding by driving alongside flowing streams and open water.

"We roll down the windows and listen. Kingfishers often stay here all year. When the leaves are gone, you can hear that rattle-y call they make much more easily."

Even easier bird watching may be pursued at almost any nature center. The E.B. Lyons Nature Center, in Dubuque, has a new indoor viewing room overlooking a well-stocked set of bird feeders.

Frozen Falls

Pikes Peak State Park in McGregor, Iowa, also maintains bird feeders at its secluded Homestead unit, as well as ungroomed ski and snowshoe trails nearby.

Park manager Matt Tschirgi used to shovel the boardwalk down to Bridal Veil Falls by hand. He stopped doing that of a couple years ago, but birders who hike that trail find elegant frozen ice falls, pile-

Tree sparrow

ated woodpeckers, white-breasted nuthatches and tufted titmice.

Meanwhile, bald eagles come and go from their roosts on the hill-sides near the overlook that juts out over the confluence of the Wisconsin and Mississippi Rivers. The path to the overlook is kept clear, Tschirgi said.

Hawks and Owls

Keeping an annual bird list provides added incentive for people like Dan Jackson, of La Crosse, Wis., to get out in the winter. Every January 1, Jackson, a member of the Coulee Region Audubon Society, restarts his bird count from zero.

His best year for La Crosse County was about 200 species. Last winter, from about December 1 to March 1, he saw 75 species of birds, of which 55 species were in the Coulee Region.

Dan's favorite place to go birding is Goose Island Park, just south of La Crosse, for three reasons: hawks, feeders and owls.

The marshy areas around Goose Island are fun places to watch for hawks. Harriers, strong, long-winged birds that fly closely over the contours of the land, don't remain in the area all winter, but they stay late and return early, Jackson said.Rough legged hawks, another of Jackson's favorites, are buteos like red-tailed hawks, but they hover

Bald eagle

in one spot and watch for prey to emerge from the snowy cover.

A set of bird feeders at the south end of the park are maintained by local birders. People come with birdseed every day, so the birds expect it.

"Some birds will even feed out of your hand there," Jackson said. "Even downy woodpeckers."

Look for great horned owls, barred owls, Eastern screech owls and sometimes long-eared owls at the edges between woods and open areas woods.

"Owls start to call a lot in January, because they're starting to mate. Watch for them at dusk," Jackson advised.

Golden and Bald Eagles

February and March are prime eagle-watching months on the Upper Mississippi. The grand birds gather in the trees and on the ice near open patches of water, such as below lock and dams.

At night, bald eagles that have fished and scavenged along the river all day head for shelter to escape brutal winter winds. They cluster together for warmth in areas called "night roosts." One of the largest night roosts in the nation is in the Milan Bottoms in the Quad Cities, where as many as 800 bald eagles gather.

"You can't see them in the woods, but you can watch them fly in there in the evening. The best place to watch is from South Concord Street in Davenport [Iowa]," said Dick Sayles of the Quad City Audubon Society. "It's adjacent to Nahant Marsh and Credit Island, and there's more good birding in both of those areas."

Lesser known are the golden eagles, which migrate down from Canada. They are larger than many bald eagles, but are a rich golden brown. Golden eagles don't eat fish, so they don't hang out by the river. Instead they cruise the second line of hills behind the river, hunting for mice and other small game that live on the goat prairies. The National Eagle Center hosts an annual census by volunteer birders, who travel assigned routes looking for golden eagles on a given day.

Birding by Boat

Ducks won't stay around on an ice-covered river, but they may not fly far south. Many diving ducks can be seen in open areas of the river from Port Byron and Hampton, Ill., down to the Quad Cities.

Quad Cities birders keep a keen eye out for crossbills, northern birds with bill tips that cross over each other, the better to tweeze seeds from seed hulls. These birds seldom make it so far south, but they have been known to frequent the Fairmount Cemetery in Davenport.

If there's snow, try cross-country skiing and watching for birds on a golf course, advised Dick Sayles. The Faukie Golf Course in Rock Island, Ill., and the old golf course on Credit Island are easy and flat enough to allow you to lift your eyes off the ground and scan the sky. These places offer splendid sights and sounds of pileated woodpeckers and red-headed woodpeckers.

Sayles is considering birding by canoe or kayak this winter, if the weather is mild. He'd like to put in by the Rock River roller dam and make his way down to the Mississippi River, to Fairport or to Buffalo Shores Recreation Area. What would he see to make it worth the cold water dripping down his sleeves?

"It probably depends on the year," he said. "But I don't like birding from a car. I prefer some adventure, and it's so beautiful out there in the backwaters."

Barred owl

Eavesdrop on the Owls of Winter

By Joan Schnabel

If you are out in the woods and someone asks about your cook, laughs maniacally then gives a blood curdling scream, you have probably encountered a pair of barred owls. (You can hear their calls, "Who cooks for you? Who cooks for you all?" on some brding websites.) Large, brown eyed owls, barred owls are one of the most common owls in our region. Often found by the river, they are the owls you are most likely to see during the day. Their name comes from the fact that the feather pattern at their almost non-existent necks runs horizontal, i.e., "barred," rather than vertical, or "streaked."

Most owls have great camouflage and don't move around much during the day, so they are difficult to spot. The standard advice is to look for pellets (the regurgitated bones, fur and feathers of small animals) and then look up, but that never works for me so I can't recommend it. The best bet is to listen for owls at dusk or at night. I hear them way more often than I see them.

If an owl inquires about your insomnia — "Who's awake? Me, too!" — you're probably listening to a great horned owl — large, yellow-eyed owls common in our area. Their "horns" are really feathers that help provide camouflage. Great horned owls are early nesters. They are sometimes on their eggs as early as January — timing that helps them usurp nests of red-tailed hawks. In their diet, great horned owls are generalists who will kill and eat almost anything, including skunks.

For the last year, I have had the pleasure of living with Galileo, a 14-year-old great horned owl. Galileo is also affectionately called "Gali," or "GB" for his pungent gopher breath. Hit by a car and blind in one eye, Gali now teaches people about raptors along with his partner, Sky, an injured red-tailed hawk. Gali is a loud hooter on most fall nights, starting around midnight. Fortunately we are blessed with tolerant neighbors. Last year GB attracted a mate into the yard, and I wondered if I should allow conjugal visits.

A whinny or trill at night is often coming from an eastern screech owl, a small owl that resembles a small great horned owl. This is one of the few species of owls with color morphs (phases) — red, gray and mixed. Northern saw-whet owls, small owls that make the sound of a truck backing up — "beep-beep-beep" — can also be heard in the woods, especially during fall migration. They don't seem to migrate farther south than Minnesota and Wisconsin.

During the winter, especially if food is scarce up north, snowy owls sometimes come visiting. Big white owls of Harry Potter fame, they are one of the few owl species to display sexual dimorphism in their plumage, with the males being more pure white and the females being more barred. Long-eared owls and short-eared owls may also be here, but are rarely seen. Barn owls, unfortunately, are no longer found in this part of their former range, although they may be found in southern Iowa and Illinois. Their decline is probably due to habitat loss and loss of the old barns whose haylofts provided fertile hunting for the barn owls.

If you'd like to learn more about owls, the International Owl Center in Houston, Minn., has a resident great horned owl and holds its International Festival of Owls the first weekend in March, offering a great opportunity to see various species. Take a winter trip to Sax-Zim Bog in northern Minnesota to see some of the northern species that are not found along the river. These include great gray owls (the biggest owl lengthwise, although snowies weigh more), northern hawk owls, and if you are very lucky, boreal owls.

If you'd like to read more, *Intriguing Owls* by Stan Tekiela is an excellent basic book with great photographs, and *North American Owls, Biology and Natural History* by Paul A. Johnsgard provides a wealth of scientific information.

Great horned owl

Eastern kingbird

Birds in January

By Pamela Eyden

I f you go to the woods at dawn or dusk in early January, you may hear the hooting of a great horned owl — a long, low, hoot, warning other owlish intruders away. This largest of all common owls is a year-round resident on the Upper Mississippi, but some drift southward in winter, and they hoot to mark their new territories.

After pairing up in early winter, great horned owls nest in tree holes abandoned by squirrels. By late January and early February, many are laying eggs.

Like other owls, they hunt from twilight to dawn, taking mostly rabbits and mice in the winter. If they don't need all the food they kill, they let it freeze and come back to thaw it out by sitting on it, much like they incubate their eggs.

With careful stalking you may catch a glimpse of a great horned owl, but your best bet is to follow the excited cawing of crows, who for reasons unknown spend a lot of time mobbing and chasing owls off their territory.

Meanwhile, other birds who are familiar sights along the Mississippi River in the summer are living very different lives in Central and South America.

One of these "Jekyll-and-Hyde" birds is the eastern kingbird. Up North, it lives alone or in pairs and eats only insects. Near the river, it's often found perching upright on snags or overhanging branches, then darting off to nab an insect out of the air before returning to its perch.

In winter, the kingbird inhabits the subtropical forests of Colombia, Chile and Argentina, where it becomes a flocking fruitarian. It travels in large flocks with other kingbirds to scout out ripening fruits and berries. Hundreds of birds move from tree to tree, feeding noisily and conspicuously, en masse, much like cedar waxwings in late summer in the North.

After crossing the Gulf of Mexico in the spring, kingbirds eat only insects again until the next winter.

Birds in February

By Pamela Eyden

Woodpeckers are the noisiest birds in the woods near the Mississippi River — especially in February, when big winds blow and the weather starts to change.

The noisiest and most conspicuous is the pileated woodpecker. This big, black bird flies in a series of swoops: first a slow, deliberate flapping, then a glide.

You may see or hear it hunting for food; it flies from one dead or diseased tree to the next, tapping experimentally and cocking its head to listen for whatever it has disturbed. When it hears something stirring, it drills a rectangular hole and extracts carpenter ants or larvae with its long, sticky tongue. This can't be an easy life. All other insect-eating birds migrate south when insects go dormant.

Pileated woodpeckers make a lot more noise in late winter. They mate for life, but every year they renew their bonds by acting out the courtship rituals again: they drum on resonant trees to mark their territory, they call to each other and chase off intruders together. Every night they shelter in their own roosting holes. Each bird has several.

Like everything else in the north woods, though, woodpeckers have to be flexible to survive the winter. Though it prefers a diet that is about 75 percent insects, it will also eat nuts, wild grapes, and

Big River Magazine, February 2001

Sandhill crane

whatever sumac, poison oak and poison ivy berries are still around. Suet mixed with nuts will draw them to bird feeders. Pileateds will even take carrion if conditions are hard enough — they've been seen eating road-kill. They're quite good at getting the marrow from bones. But the same desperation that drives the hungry pileated woodpecker into the open also makes it vulnerable to attack by hawks, which are its only real predators.

Meanwhile, the satellites that track migratory birds reveal that they, too, get restless in early February. Ospreys tracked by the University of Minnesota Raptor Center start moving around in the hills of Colombia

Sandhill cranes leave their winter digs on the Gulf Coast of Texas and start moving north. By late February or early March they settle in along the Platte River of Nebraska by the hundreds of thousands, gleaning corn left in fields and roosting in the river shallows at night. If they time it right, they will return to the streams and backwaters of the Mississippi in March to find the ice melted and the frogs and crawfish coming to life again.

Osprey

Birds in March

By Pamela Eyden

Gizzard shad, one of the most plentiful fish in the Mississippi River, have a hard time toward the end of a long, cold winter. In the summer shad eat algae, following it as it gets blown about by the wind, which makes them easy prey for osprey and other fishing birds. In the fall, when the algae dies off, the shad feed on detritus — decaying bits of plants and animals.

If the ice freezes around them or they don't get enough to eat, they die and become detritus themselves. Or they bob to the surface to provide an easy meal for hungry eagles. Eagles are carrion-eaters, preferring dead fish to live ones. This time of year, they gather below dams or along leads that open up in frozen backwaters, watching for fish. They hover like gulls, play with their food and fight over it.

Observers have counted as many as 500 eagles jockeying for position on the ice at Trempealeau National Wildlife Refuge. Eagle-watching may be even better there this year, because the U.S. Fish and Wildlife Service lowered water levels there last fall and many spots froze solid to the bottom.

An increasing number of bald eagles are building nests in the Upper Mississippi River Valley and staying around all year. In March, they court and stake out territory. Watch the blufftops. You may see them chasing each other, locking talons and tumbling in a

free fall. They may be pals, siblings, prospective mates and sometimes all of the above.

But most bald eagles go north to mate, nest and raise their young.
The University of Minnesota Raptor Center has tracked several bald
eagles from wintering grounds on the Mississippi between Iowa and
Illinois to nesting places in Canada. By early March they're at the
U.S.-Canada border, well on their way.

Meanwhile, just as the eagles are leaving, osprey are returning
from Mexico, Central America and South America.

The Raptor Center also tracks osprey. A female called "ZO" has
spent the last two winters near Lake Maracaibo, in Venezuela. She
left there on March 16 last year and flew over Colombia, Panama and
Costa Rica in four days, then across Nicaragua, Honduras, Guatemala and around the Gulf of Mexico in another eight days. She was
in Waukon, Iowa, by April 6, and "home" in the Twin Cities area by
April 8. It took her just 23 days to fly 4,000-plus miles.

Osprey tend to be very faithful to specific places in both summer
and winter.

"My guess is they go back to the same trees every year," said
Mark Martell, Raptor Center project manager. "They're familiar with
the area — they know the good hunting spots, they know the safe
places to sleep at night, and they know their neighbors, which means
there would be fewer territorial disputes."

Osprey are faithful to the same mates, but they don't stay together
all year. ZO's mate, "B4," winters in Chiapas, Mexico. Their two off-
spring from the summer of 1999 have been in Panama and Colombia
for the past 18 months. Young osprey usually don't return north their
first year.

Although osprey eat live fish and bald eagles prefer dead ones,
there may be some competition between the two birds. According to
the Wisconsin Department of Natural Resources, the number of
osprey nests in 40 counties decreased from 403 in 1998 to 384 in 1999.
They speculate that the two birds may be just similar enough in their
territory and nest site preferences that an increase in one could cause
a decrease in the other.

Birds in April

By Pamela Eyden

Timing is everything in the spring, especially in April when the first leaves open.

One spring I went walking in a grove of cottonwoods, looking for birds, but there weren't many. The Arizona trees seemed to have lost their leaves. I felt bad, suspecting poison or disease. Later, the landowners told me a different story: the cottonwoods had sprouted new leaves as usual, but no sooner had the leaves opened than tent caterpillars appeared to eat them — so many caterpillars that my friends had to wear hats to protect themselves, not from dropping caterpillars but from caterpillar droppings. Soon, a wave of migratory birds had appeared on the scene. They feasted on the caterpillars for several days until there were no more, then the birds left, too.

Arriving late, I'd missed the whole show. All I'd seen were bare trees, and I hadn't even interpreted them right. Timing is everything!

If you go walking along the Mississippi River in the spring, you'll notice that willow leaves are among the first to open. They open earlier along the Mississippi than in other places nearby, because of the warming effect of the water. If you turn over the small leaves and find the backsides nibbled away, leaving the top surface intact, you are looking at the work of willowleaf beetles. They are among the first insects out and about in the spring.

Big River Magazine, April 2001

Tree swallow

Many species of leaf beetles live on the willows, alders and cottonwoods along the river. They are an important source of food for migratory birds — those that rest here temporarily on their journeys farther north and those that nest here, such as warblers, swallows and swifts.

Six of the eight species of swallows in the U.S. live in the Upper Mississippi region. They winter in different places and have different migration behavior, but none return north until the insects are out.

Tree swallows, for example, are usually the earliest swallow. They winter in the southern states, Mexico, Guatemala and Cuba. They start arriving in the Upper Mississippi Valley from late March through early May. The peak of their migration occurs in mid-April, according to Robert Janssen's *Birds in Minnesota*.

Purple martins, on the other hand, leave their Amazon Basin wintering grounds in January. They fly north across the Gulf of Mexico and hang out on the Gulf coast until the North warms up. About eight million purple martins migrate through Louisiana. Crowds of martin watchers on Lake Pontchartrain sometimes create crowd-control problems for New Orleans. Purple martins may arrive in the Upper Mississippi River Valley anytime from late March through mid-May, depending on the weather.

Chimney swifts are another insect-eating bird that often returns in April. Swifts are sometimes confused with swallows, but they don't hold their tails in a V-shape, as do swallows, and are said to look like "cigars with wings." Tail or no tail, swifts are among the fastest birds. They spend winters near rivers in the tropical lowland forests of the Amazon basin of Peru. Migrating north in the spring, they fly continuously, sometimes 500 miles a day, until they cross the Gulf of Mexico. From that point on, they take their time, letting the season unfold as they move north.

It's great fun to watch these aerobatic birds, as they swoop and dive to hunt for insects. They do this by flying fast with their mouths open and scooping insects out of the air. They also bathe, court their mates and do almost everything in the air, including taking fly-by sips from the surface of the river.

By late May, swifts, like many other birds, have finished their courtship, built their nests and started raising families. They're quieter and busier.

Don't miss the dramas of April.

Cerulean warbler

Birds in May

By Pamela Eyden

Cerulean warblers are some of the most beautiful birds in the Upper Mississippi River Valley. Only a few inches long, the males are bright blue above and white below, with a dark line across the throat and two white bars on the wing. Females are pale blue-green on top and pale yellow below. Ceruleans are hard to find, though. They stay for only a short time (10 to 12 weeks), build their nests in the canopy of the tallest trees and live in large tracts of bottomland forest.

"They're usually two miles in, through nettles, mud and mosquitoes," said Winona birder Richie Swanson, who has walked many miles monitoring cerulean nests since 1992. He wrote about his project in "Down But Not Out," which was published in *Birder's World* (12(3): 28-31, 1998).

Males arrive by early May and sing to compete for nesting territory. Swanson said their songs are a soft "twee-twee-twee-tweez" — hard to hear over the rustle of cottonwood leaves. Females arrive two weeks later, choose mates and build nests. By August the young have fledged and grown, and they head back to South America for the winter.

Ceruleans are harder to find now than they were 20 years ago. According to Breeding Bird Survey data, their numbers may be

Big River Magazine, May 2001

declining faster than any other warbler in North America, about four percent per year. In the Mississippi Valley, bottomland forests are being fragmented and tall trees are not regenerating because of high water and the growth of reed canary grass. In South America, ceruleans winter on the eastern flanks of the Andes Mountains between 1,600 and 4,800 feet — exactly where new coffee, cacao, tea and other plantations have been clearing forests in recent decades.

Traditional coffee plantations are shady places that provide fairly good habitat for resident and migratory birds. But coffee is now the world's second largest agricultural commodity, after cotton. In the last 10 years, according to Conservation International, 40 percent of the traditional coffee fields in Mexico, Colombia, Central America and the Caribbean were converted to treeless, chemical-intensive plantations growing new, sun-tolerant coffee varieties.

"Shade-Grown Coffee" is the theme of International Migratory Bird Day on May 12 this year. It makes a difference what you drink. Most organic coffee is shade-grown. For more information, visit the Partners in Flight website.

Birds are not the only winged creatures returning in May and June. Monarch butterflies fly to Mexico every fall, and their descendants return in the spring.

Dragonflies migrate, too. The first ones you see in May are common green darners. These are the children or grandchildren of the ones that left last fall. They'll mate right away, then three months later the next generation will emerge and fly south. Dragonflies fly under the same weather conditions and use the same routes as birds do. In fact, common green darners are counted along with migrating kestrels at Duluth's Hawk Ridge Nature Reserve in September.

A second population of common green darners stick around during the winter. This non-migratory population emerges from larva in June or July, and they look just like the migratory population.

Paddling for Birds on the Mississippi

By Tom Watson

S omeone once observed that you can see more wildlife during a day of kayaking than you can in a week of hiking. That person must have been birding on the Mississippi River.

A birder for over 15 years in Alaska, I returned to the Upper Mississippi with an impressive "life list" of birds I had seen there. I doubled my list in only one year of paddling in the channels and backwaters of the mighty river.

The backwaters are a treasure trove of species, from sandpipers and peepers flitting along the sandbars and flood flats, to herons, egrets and other stilt legs probing the shorelines, to massive flocks of coots, to kettles of pelicans, to magnificent "Vs" of migrating tundra swans, to countless songbirds. Because over 40 percent of the birds that migrate through North America use the Mississippi River corridor, even a beginner can expect scores of sightings daily. Those opportunities are even greater if you're watching birds from a kayak or canoe.

Paddling a boat that drafts only a few inches of water gives you access to a variety of backwaters — whether it's a shallow, reed-lined marsh between towering bluffs and the Main Channel, clusters of

White pelicans

sandbars or an expansive shallow pool behind one of the dams. The waters of the Mississippi are often connected in networks that extend for miles, with marshes leading to narrow channels that lead to expansive open lakes that connect with dead-end sloughs.

The U.S. Fish and Wildlife Service produces very good, small, free maps of the river from Wabasha, Minn., to the Quad Cities. Also free, the *Mississippi River Companion*, published by the National Park Service, contains detailed maps of 72 miles of river in the Twin Cities, from just downriver of Elk River, Minn., to just upriver of Diamond Bluff, Wis.

Opportunity most often comes from patient waiting or slow and deliberate approaches. A small gliding boat with a shallow draft enables you to get incredibly close to birds. A good pair of binoculars (8x42 to 10x50 is a popular range) and a telephoto lens (200 to 300mm) can bring you face-to-bill with most species. While compact binoculars are often praised for being lightweight and convenient, a heavier pair will be easier to hold steady while bobbing around in even the most stable boats. Whatever equipment you choose, being waterproof is essential. Waterproof cases are great for transporting gear, but you sometimes need a quick-draw with the shutter as opportunities literally take off right in front of you.

White pelicans have incredible wingspans, nearly 10 feet long. They sometimes glide effortlessly like a string of boxcars just above the surface as they move from one area to the other.

As I cautiously approached the edge of a large flock one summer afternoon in a backwater lake near Trempealeau, Wis., the flock suddenly decided to stretch their broad wings and lift off the surface of the water on a path that took them directly over me. Dozens of the magnificent birds streamed past my kayak, some gliding by less than the length of their wings above me. The methodic beat of their powerful wings filled the air with a mesmerizing swooshing sound unlike anything I had ever heard.

To optimize your viewing success, prepare for what you might see and what type of habitat you might find it in. I have several expansive identification guidebooks that I study religiously at home before and after an outing, but I take a smaller pocket guide with me to the field. Colorful art plates are helpful, but photographs are usually better at revealing the shades and hues you will see in the wild. Some plumages, such as shades of red and even a medium blue, can look gray to black in the shade or backlit. If you know the general

Solitary sandpiper

make-up of the landscape you'll be exploring, you can study up on the birds you can expect to see there.

It's also very important to know the migration, reproductive and rearing seasons of species. Access to some areas is restricted during waterfowl migration, breeding and/or nesting times.

Knowing the behavior of birds can help you determine your approach and, if you are a photographer, how much time you'll have before they burst into flight. Treat every hidden turn and blind shoreline as a potential opportunity for an encounter.

One day I was slicing my kayak bow through six-foot-high marsh rushes and cattails as I literally pulled my boat through a shallow flood wash between two islands in a backwater slough when I heard the guttural yodeling call of a sandhill crane. I was anxious to see if I could get a view of the small flock I had spotted on previous visits. My approach was as silent as paper-dry blades of grass scraping my kayak would allow.

When I came to the edge of a floating sedge raft surrounded by a thick, fence-like barricade of reeds, I paused then braced myself and made a forceful lunge to thrust the bow forward. Sunlight disappeared in a thunderous beating of wings and rustling of reeds as four sandhills exploded skyward out of the center of the small, floating island.

Most encounters are much more subtle.

Being quiet and limiting your movements or just drifting usually enables you to get surprisingly close to even some of the more cautious and elusive birds. A kayak's low profile makes it especially good for approaches — they were, after all, designed to be hunting boats. Developing a lower paddling stroke can decrease your visibility. Paddle motion and the glint of sunlight off a wet paddle can spook critters from a long distance away.

Most wildlife viewing is best right after dawn and during the golden glow of dusk. Below the steep Mississippi River bluffs the sun sets much earlier. Subdued light usually doesn't affect viewing as much as it can affect exposures, even with digital cameras.

Maintaining a low profile in your boat, approaching slowly and having patience all make for successful bird watching. Clunking paddles against the canoe's gunwales or slapping the water with each stroke will send a signal to already cautious creatures.

Spring floods are a double-edged sword: treacherous floodwaters hold eddies and hidden obstructions that can be deceptive and dangerous, but high water also creates opportunities to paddle into places that are inaccessible during the summer. Some areas behind dikes are flooded but have very little current during high water. Cautious journeys through these floodwaters can reward you with wildlife encounters you'd never have from a motorboat.

As they say: It's the journey and not the destination that is important. Bird watching on the Mississippi from a canoe or kayak offers a satisfying proof of that.

Snow geese

Favorite Fall Birding Spots on the Upper Mississippi

By Pamela Eyden

Okay, you were busy. You had a great time birding last spring, but then your thoughts turned to other things — work, school, elections, national scandals, the stock market. Now you wake up on Saturday with a sinking feeling that it's too late: the bluebirds, rose-breasted grosbeaks and purple martins are all gone. Is there any reason to get out of bed and go off into the wild blue yonder with binocs around your neck?

Yes!

Fall is a great time to go birding in the Mississippi River Valley. As one of the continent's four main migration flyways, it is full of ducks and geese from September through November, when the river starts freezing up. You'll find them diving and dabbling in shallow backwaters and protected bays from the Twin Cities to the Quad Cities. There are dozens of different kinds, and they're easy to identify and study this time of year. Pintails, buffleheads, ring-necks and mergansers — soon you, too, will have a favorite duck. Take your bird book and a folding chair.

Big River Magazine, October 1998

Hawks migrate by the thousands along the blufftops, especially on clear, high-pressure days with winds out of the north and northwest. Try any of the bluff-top parks all along the river. It's an awesome sight that reminds you how lucky you are to live here.

You'll find a lot of bald eagles along the river, too. Some are permanent residents; others have come down from up north to take advantage of plentiful fish in the open water below dams and at the confluences of rivers.

Don't let November end without making a trip to see the tundra swans, which stop to rest and feed here on their way from the Arctic to the Chesapeake Bay on the East Coast. Groups of these great white birds can be found almost anywhere from Lake Pepin to Ferryville, Wis., but for large numbers go to Rieck's Lake near Alma, Wis. [Editors note: As of 2018, Brownsville, Minn., had become the best place to see large numbers of tundra swans in the fall.]

Trumpeter swans, the largest waterfowl in the world, are a striking sight on the upper river, and can be found year round at several Hennepin County parks in the Twin Cities.

The weather in fall is more unpredictable and variable than at any other time of the year. Birds know it. Their excitement is audible and visible, from the anxious twittering of the last goldfinches on the sunflowers, to the miles-long rivers of blackbirds streaming over the fields, to the hypnotic conversations of ducks, geese and swans in the marshes. Students of migration have a word for the migratory restlessness that comes over birds this time of year — "zugunruhe." Even captive birds show it, and I think (the smartest) people do, too.

Sites to See

Chippewa National Forest, Grand Rapids, Minn.
The Mississippi headwaters has the largest nesting population of bald eagles in the lower 48 states. Many stay all year; others migrate south in late fall. Check out the river and the larger lakes in the area — Cass, Reeds and Winnibigoshish.

Monticello to Elk River, Minn.
This ten-mile stretch of the river stays ice-free all winter because of warm water flushed from the nuclear power plant. Last year 280 trumpeter swans arrived in November and stayed until March. Eagles hang around, too.

Coon Rapids Dam Regional Park, Anoka, Minn.

Watch for bald eagles below the dam, and for golden-eyes, which arrive in November and stay all winter in between the islands.

Minnesota Valley National Wildlife Refuge

This refuge near the confluence of the Minnesota and Mississippi Rivers is worth returning to several times in the fall, because the population of migrants changes constantly.

Battle Creek Regional Park, St. Paul

On the east side of the Mississippi River across from downtown St. Paul, this wooded ravine provides protection for late-flying migratory birds. The Minnesota Ornithological Union sponsors a tour there in late September.

Bay City and Stockholm, Wis.

Late fall brings thousands of common mergansers to Lake Pepin to rest and feed. Keep your eyes peeled for these striking, black-and-white headed birds.

Buena Vista Park, Alma

A bluff-top park that lifts you several hundred feet closer to the hawks that migrate with favorable winds out of the north. (If the winds are out of the south, stay home. The hawks will, too.)

Kellogg Weaver Dunes Scientific and Natural Area, Kellogg, Minn.

The Weaver Dunes and the McCarthy Lake Wildlife Management Area together make up thousands of acres of sand prairies, oak savannas and wet meadows bordering the Mississippi southeast of Wabasha — good hunting grounds for hungry hawks migrating in late September through October and cover for a mix of sparrows and other migratory birds.

Prairie Island, Winona, Minn.

Saved by the local bird club from its sorry status as an unofficial town-dump, this restored-prairie is now a great place to see eagles, osprey and migrating waterfowl, warblers and sparrows (chipping, clay-colored, field, fox, grasshopper, Lincoln's, savannah, song, swamp, tree, vesper, white-throated and white-crowned).

Trempealeau National Wildlife Refuge, Trempealeau, Wis.

Named one of the world's most important bird areas by the Ameri-

Chipping sparrow

can Bird Conservancy, this refuge has a new visitor center and an observation deck with spotting scopes that make it easy to watch great numbers of ducks, geese, cormorants and tundra swans, as well as bald eagles and osprey.

Long Lake Canoe Trail, south of Trempealeau, Wis.

This four-mile trail includes quiet backwater sloughs, dense wooded islands and a bit of the Main Channel. Autumn bird-watching is excellent, but canoeists should avoid disturbing the rafts of water-fowl that may be gathering in the Big Marsh. Watch for cormorants!

Hixon Forest Nature Center, La Crosse, Wis.

Try the River-to-Bluff Trail, which starts at Riverside Park on the Mississippi, traverses the great La Crosse River Marsh and then up the bluff, all without crossing a single street.

Goose Island Park, La Crosse, Wis.

The canoe trail is closed from Oct 1 to Nov. 15 because so many ducks, geese and shorebirds stop here to rest and feed. But you can hike the trails and watch from shore. (Watch out for poison ivy, which is at its most potent this time of year.)

Black Hawk Park, De Soto, Wis.

This large park is very busy on weekends, but the two boat ramps give direct access to a complicated set of islands, sloughs and backwaters.

Hwy. 35 between Ferryville and Lynxville, Wis.

Canvasbacks used to disperse all along the river on their way south, but now they concentrate in Pool 9 because their favorite food, wildcelery, is plentiful. There are pull-overs on the highway and an observation deck at the south end of Ferryville. Beginning in late October, hundreds of tundra swans rest and feed in Pool 9, also.

Yellow River State Forest, Harpers Ferry, Iowa

A large forest with several accessible units, including the Paint Creek Unit on Big Paint Creek and the Luster Heights Unit where the Little Paint Creek enters the Mississippi. These wooded lands are nesting grounds of hawks and also shelter migratory birds of all kinds

Effigy Mounds National Monument, Marquette, Iowa

Great views of the river valley below and a great place to watch for hawks.

Wyalusing State Park, south of Prairie du Chien, Wis.

The park's bird list cites flycatchers, a variety of sandpipers and the rufous-sided towhee as autumn visitors, besides screech, horned and barred owls. The canoe trail offers a chance to see lots of waterfowl. The bluffs are good places to check for red-shouldered hawks and other migrating raptors.

Turkey River Bottoms, south of Guttenberg, Iowa

Fall visitors include wood ducks, green- and blue-winged teal, black ducks, mallards, shovelers, wigeons, canvasbacks, ring-necks, lesser scaups, common golden-eyes, buffleheads, and hooded and comon mergansers.

Nelson Dewey State Park, Cassville, Wis.

This park occupies the steep bluffs above the river and is a good place to watch migrating hawks, eagles and turkey vultures.

Bertom Lake, near Cassville

Depending on how high or low the water is, you can hike quite a

Hooded merganser

ways in from the road at the Bertom Lake area, south of Cassville. One of the few places where you can get into the refuge on foot. (Watch out for poison ivy!)

New Albin, Iowa
Army Road leads to a boat landing and is surrounded by marshes and protected sloughs — likely hide-outs for migratory waterfowl.

Eagle Point Park, Dubuque, Iowa
This park has precipitous views of the river and spacious lawns upon which to lie, watching for migrating eagles, raptors and turkey vultures.

Mines of Spain State Recreation Area, Dubuque, Iowa
A lush, protected stopover for migratory birds.

Lock and Dam 14 Eagle Area, Bettendorf, Iowa
Eagles stay all year in this eight-acre Nature Conservancy preserve near Bettendorf. A Bald Eagle count map is available.

Birds on the Move During Fall Migration

Canvasback ducks

Canvasbacks nest in the prairie marshes and potholes of the Dakotas, and spend winters in the lower Mississippi Valley. During migration, watch for them in Lake Onalaska and Pool 9, where they feed on the still-plentiful aquatic plant, wild celery.

Double-crested cormorants

Double-crested cormorants resemble big black ducks with longish necks. They nest on the Upper Mississippi and migrate as far south as west central Mexico, the Bahamas and the Greater Antilles. They fly in groups, sometimes right above the surface of the water.

Osprey

Also called fish-hawks, these fast-flying diving birds migrate like other hawks along the bluff tops. They spend the winter in Chile and northern Argentina.

Broad-winged hawk

Broad-wings, with their boldly striped black-and-white tails, are easy to identify. They migrate in great numbers down the Mississippi River Valley, preferring days with north or northwesterly tailwinds to push them along. They ascend in thermals, spiraling up together in a kind of whirlwind of hawks, called a kettle, and then glide smoothly along the ridge tops until they find another thermal. They mass in southern Texas, then continue on to Central and South America.

Semipalmated sandpiper

Watch for sandpipers in mudflats or in sandy shallow-water marshes. They migrate in flocks of 20 to 100 from their nesting grounds in the High Arctic to their wintering places in Panama and South America.

Snow goose

This goose is nicknamed the blue goose because the young have remarkably blue-gray feathers. Their breeding grounds are on Baffin and Southampton Islands in the Arctic. Most spend the winter in Louisiana's coastal marshes. Watch for them feeding in shallow pools of the river.

Semipalmated sandpiper

Tundra swans

Formerly called whistling swans, they fly with necks out straight.
Spend summers on south Baffin Island and the northern Arctic sea-
coast, then fly a dog-leg course to the Mississippi River Valley and on
to wintering grounds on the Chesapeake Bay. High concentrations of
tundra swans rest and feed in the Upper Mississippi in the fall — an
estimated 15,000 of them between Alma and Genoa, Wis.

Trumpeter swans

Trumpeter swans were once common in Minnesota and all of North
America. Hunting, then DDT, nearly did them in by the 1960s. Now
they're making a comeback. Find them all year at parks in the Twin
Cities (call Hennepin County Parks for specific information). They
sometimes also migrate with other waterfowl, especially tundra
swans.

Turkey vultures

These eagle-sized birds with "fingered" wing tips often begin migrating in August, but may still be here as late as November, depending
on the weather.

Aerial view of tundra swans (UMESC)

Bird Science

Cruising for a Bird's Eye View of Ducks, Geese and Swans.. 181

Soaring with the Dinosaurs 187

National Birdhood: Eagle? Or Turkey? 193

179

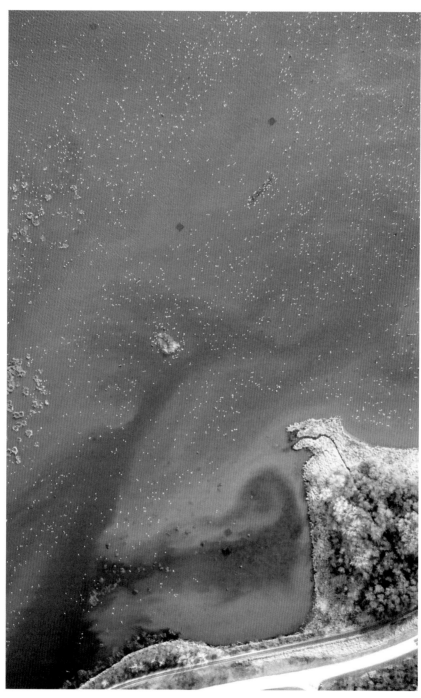

Tundra swans eating arrowhead tubers in Pool 8, 2004. (UMESC)

Cruising for a Bird's Eye View of Ducks, Geese and Swans

By Pamela Eyden

At the end of September, 2,238 migrating Canada geese and 10,610 migrating ducks were visiting the Upper Mississippi River National Wildlife and Fish Refuge, according to the refuge website.

Those of us who stand on the shore watching and listening to the tides of migratory birds in the fall may wonder who counts all those birds. After all, birds are wild! They're free! How can anyone know how many tundra swans, Canada geese, canvasbacks, pintails, scaups, mallards and other ducks are on the 261 miles (240,000 acres) of the Upper Mississippi River Refuge?

Counting Heads

Every Tuesday morning from late September through November, a pilot and and two biologists take off from the Winona, Minn., airport and fly upriver to Pool 4, where they begin their day's work, counting waterfowl.

Big River Magazine, November-December 2005

They fly low and slow, cruising at 80 to 90 knots at an altitude of 150 feet over the water, retracing the same path from pools 4 through 13. The twin-engine Partavia airplane is well suited to this job — its wings extend from the top of the cabin, like a Cessna's, and the front of the plane is all window, like a helicopter.

"It's a cramped airplane, and it gets hot in there if the sun is out, but it's a fantastic view of the river," said Bill Thrune, U.S. Fish and Wildlife Service (F&WS) biologist who has done aerial surveys here for more than ten years.

It takes six or seven hours to fly the route, then another few hours to transcribe the numbers back in the office. Flying is the more exciting part of the job.

"We do get keyed up for it. There's a lot going on out there. And if you have shear winds off the bluffs, it gets really exciting!" said Eric Nelson, F&WS biologist who flew aerial surveys from 1991 to 2001.

One observer sits in the front on the right; the second observer sits in back on the left. They count all the birds they see within an eighth mile on each side of the plane.

"We count the wings and divide by two," Nelson joked.

In reality, like ground observers, they gauge a group of 50 or 100 birds, then expand outward to estimate how many such groups there are.

"We look out at a spot on the wing or the motor and use it as a gauge to say, 'There's a block of 1,000. There's 2,000. There's 3,000.' All the time, we're talking into our own microphones, tape recording what we see," said Nelson.

Wherever vast numbers of birds gather, such as on Lake Onalaska in Pool 7, observers may estimate the total number, then note they saw "about 60 percent canvasbacks and 30 percent scaups."

In early October, wood ducks, teals and wigeons arrive, along with pelicans, cormorants and eagles. In mid-October, large numbers of mallards start to appear, followed by canvasbacks. Tundra swans and Canada geese arrive about the same time, and that's when the counting starts to get tough. In the middle of November, observers fly over huge masses of migratory water birds.

By November they've had weeks of practice. That's a good thing, Nelson said, because when tundra swans mix with smaller birds, the eye tends to isolate the big white objects, ignoring the smaller dark ones, or vice versa. It's hard to see both at the same time.

Accuracy is important, although the count is never 100 percent accurate. "That's why we want the same aircraft, the same pilots and observers from year to year. That way we keep the same biases," Nelson said.

It's a source of pride to Nelson and others that independent sources have verified the numbers several times. In 1997, the state of Wisconsin independently counted 80,000 migratory waterfowl in Pool 9 a few hours after F&WS had counted 78,000. In 2004, the U.S. Geological Survey also videotaped the birds and counted them on screen, which also verified the accuracy of F&WS counts.

Why Count 'em?

Waterfowl counts take top priority in the fall, partly because about 40 percent of the continent's waterfowl migrate through the refuge every year, and it's the the F&WS's responsibility to "conserve and manage" migratory birds.

The agency has done aerial surveys since the 1940s. Although transects and ways of analyzing data have changed some, the decades of data tells a story of striking changes in the river and in the birds that come here.

Counts in the 1920s and 1930s, before the locks and dams were built, showed that migratory birds stayed mostly along the Main Channel and the larger side channels, because many backwater sloughs and ponds dried out by the fall. Greater scaups were the most common migrator.

After locks and dams were built, the new marshes created by higher water levels attracted great numbers of "puddle ducks," such as mallards, that eat tubers and little microinvertebrates in shallow water. (You can identify a "puddle duck" by its tail in the air and its head under water.) In 1956, there were about 200,000 mallards here, and only about 10,000 canvasback ducks.

By the mid-1970s, though, the figures had flip-flopped. Canvasbacks far outnumbered the mallards.

"Three quarters of the use of the river in the fall is by canvasbacks now," Nelson said. "That's a reflection of how the habitat on the river has changed. We've seen a general decline in puddle duck habitat. There's a lot of open water now and less emergent plants."

Canvasback ducks are "diving ducks." They are built to swim under water, and can easily dive to find food at greater depth.

Whither the Swans?

If you ask tourists and birders which migratory bird they most want to watch in the fall, they're likely to say tundra swans. Yet swans don't appear at all in the records of aerial surveys in the 1940s. Only a few appear in the 1950s. Observers in the 1960s counted about 100 or so. In the 1970s there were a few thousand. These days, the count is up to 35,000.

The increase seems to reflect an increase in the total number of tundra swans that migrate across the United States. They stop over in the Upper Mississippi because of its lush vegetation, specifically the arrowhead, an emergent plant with a nutritious tuber that is easily dug up by long-necked swans. But now the tubers aren't where they used to be. Rieck's Lake in Pool 4 and Weaver Bottoms in Pool 5 have both been overwhelmed by sediment washing down from tributary rivers, burying the arrowhead. Swans still come, but they tend to congregate in greater numbers farther south, in Pool 8.

Celery Eaters

Aerial surveyors sit up and take a deep breath when approaching pools 7, 8 and 9, which host the largest numbers of migratory birds. They also contain the most food for the birds, such as wild celery and fingernail clams, and effective "closed areas."

Wild celery, arrowhead, fingernail clams and other food change from year to year, depending on river conditions. The drought of the late 1980s, for example, killed off a lot of the nutritious plants. That made life easier for fingernail clams, which then be came much more abundant. Fingernail clams aren't as nutritious as tubers, but diving ducks can get by on them. So the drought favored diving ducks.

In recent years habitat projects and drawdowns have succeeded in restoring wild celery, which should attract increasing numbers of mallards and other puddle ducks.

Stepping Stones

Aerial surveyors know they'll find more birds in closed areas than in areas that are open to hunting. Birds, like other creatures, hang out in places where there is both food, and peace and quiet to enjoy it.

Closed areas are off-limits to hunters, although fishermen and canoeists are not prohibited.

"Sometimes we'll approach a place where lots of birds have set down, but suddenly they're all in the air before we get there," Nelson said. "When we look around to see what's spooked them, it's usually someone in a boat, going right through the middle of the birds.

"There's no real sanctuary here, except for Spring Lake in Pool 13. The closed areas were established to give the birds a place to rest and feed. That's very important for migrating birds. The closed areas are like stepping stones on their way, and they work well, as long as the closed areas are productive areas."

Geese, swans and ducks need to eat well and build up their fat reserves while they are in the Upper Mississippi. Difficulty finding food here affects waterfowl populations year round.

"If they have difficulties finding food and they leave here in poor shape, they often spend the winter trying to catch up," said Thrune. "Then when they migrate back through here in the spring, they're still in poor shape. That usually means they have smaller broods the next year."

Smaller broods means fewer ducks come through the next fall.

Weekly aerial surveys are used to figure the total number of "use days" for different pools and the refuge as a whole. "Use days" is the number of birds present, multiplied by the number of days they stay here. The F&WS is interested in both the trends and the distribution of birds throughout the refuge.

For example, closed areas of the refuge accounted for 48 percent to 73 percent of the total duck "use days" from 2000 to 2003 — far more than average — according to F&WS reports.

Aerial surveys sometimes reveal changes in the numbers or locations of birds, changes that call for some biological detective work.

"If there's a lack of birds in any area, we find out why, or if birds are bunching up in an area, this is a concern," Nelson said. Usually, he said, they can trace it back to a change in habitat.

Informing the public about bird populations and migrations is an important part of the refuge biologists' job. Telephone calls and other inquiries have increased so much, the refuge now posts the numbers on a website.

"People really are interested. Birders want to know, and hunters plan their vacations around when the birds are arriving," said Nelson.

This fossil of an **Archaeopteryx** *shows marks left by feathers. (Kent Condie and Robert Sloan)*

Soaring with the Dinosaurs
Young eagles remind us of the evolution of flight

By Robert E. Sloan

Now that my wife and I are both retired, we spend a lot of time looking out our windows at the Mississippi and its inhabitants near Homer, Minnesota. Last winter into early spring we watched eagles, since there are three nests within two miles of our house.

In late February and early March we could see white heads showing above the edge of the nest nearest to our home, so we knew something was up. Finally, in mid-April, we could see the occasional black head of a hatchling stretching above the nest. In the last week of April we spotted a fledgling standing on the edge of the nest, clearly gathering courage for the big jump. By May 1, a fledgling was sitting on a branch eight feet from the nest. For the next week we both were laughing at their early, clumsy attempts at flight and soaring.

By the end of the week we were watching six of them that had discovered thermals, the rising air currents that come up from the floor of the valley. They could find thermals and stay in them, soar-

Big River Magazine, September-October 2002

ing lazy circles in the sky, except for some occasional furious flapping. They had not yet developed the precise control of the primary flight feathers on the tips of their wings. We watched one at low altitude flapping with one wing and soaring with the other. Of course, it immediately made a sharp turn, almost turned upside down and dropped — a clear oops! In a few days they were skilled enough to try fishing.

These babies must learn it all based only on instinct and lots of practice. Watching the young eagles reminded me of what we have learned about the curious evolutionary path that led to the development of birds and flight.

From Dinos to Birds

To a casual observer, a *Tyrannosaurus rex* and a canary don't seem to have much in common. Birds learned to fly and developed all the other modern bird behaviors gradually, many before they became birds. Paleontologists studying the fossil record have discovered that all dinosaurs had many bird behaviors. Jack Horner, a paleontologist at Montana State University, showed that big, plant-eating dinosaurs took care of their young, feeding them for several weeks so they could grow from 16 inches to four feet long before they left the nest. Mark Norell, curator of the American Museum of Natural History, found two specimens of mother dinosaurs — six-foot-long carnivores — that were busily brooding their eggs on a nest exactly as birds do, when they were suddenly buried in a sandstorm.

Peter Dodson of the University of Pennsylvania showed that another group of dinosaurs had distinctive vocal calls so they could easily distinguish their own kind. The upshot of all this is that dinosaurs were far more like birds than the various modern kinds of reptiles, and not all dinosaurs became extinct when the asteroid hit 65 million years ago. Birds—from eagles to ostriches to hummingbirds — are actually the most successful and varied branch of the dinosaur family!

Looking for Feathers

Part of the problem in tracing the development of birds is the fact that fossilized feathers are very rare. Fragile feathers rarely turn into fossils, because they usually rot before they are fossilized. But once in a great while, we find a place where feathers were preserved.

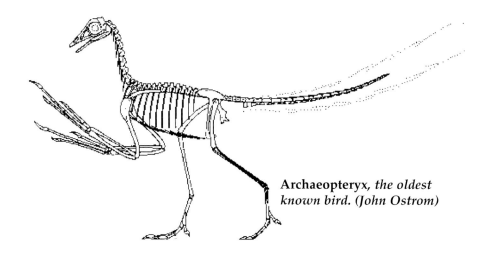

Archaeopteryx, *the oldest known bird. (John Ostrom)*

In the last 10 years paleontologists have found a great series of lake deposits in northeastern China that preserved feathers well. Fossils from these deposits include both early birds with proper, short tails, some with teeth, and others that have horny beaks. They also found long-tailed raptors with both down and cover feathers.

Some raptors known to have feathers did not fly. And only one of the feathered dinosaurs became the ancestor of birds, but others lasted quite a while longer as dinosaurs.

We now have many examples of the stages in the development of feathers themselves. Big dinosaurs had no problem keeping their body temperature constant and high; because of their great bulk they did not cool rapidly. Babies or small adult dinosaurs needed insulation to stay warm and active, and so they developed feathers. Several small (pigeon-sized) raptor dinosaurs have single or multiple hairs, instead of scales. Others went on to branched hairs similar to down. Still others were covered in proper feathers smaller than flight feathers, even on their arms.

Finding the Early Bird

Part of the question of how dinosaurs became birds was answered by my old friend, John Ostrom, a professor of paleontology at Yale and a former director of the Peabody Museum. He discovered a fossil called *Deinonychus* (dee-in-nonny-kuss), an eight-foot-long, raptor-like dinosaur in Montana.

The common meaning of the word 'raptor' refers to a bird of prey; but in Latin it means 'to seize,' and *Deinonychus* nearly fits both senses of the word. *Deinonychus* was a bird-like dinosaur with feathers and a wishbone, but it had a long dinosaur tail and teeth instead of a horny bill. It also had a bigger brain and eyes than other raptor-like dinosaurs. What made *Deinonychus* different was its very long wing-like arms with grasping, hand-like claws with three 'fingers' and an opposable 'thumb.' *Deinonychus* could not fly, but it used its arms while running, to help it gain speed and seize its prey with its claws. *Deinonychus* was part of a family of similar animals called *Maniraptors* (pronounced man-ih-rap-tors), meaning literally hand-raptors, because they have an opposable thumb. The *Velociraptor* of *Jurassic Park* is probably the most famous of the *Maniraptors*.

Ostrom was the first person to note the very detailed similarity of the *Maniraptors* to the oldest fossil birds. On a trip to Europe to examine fossils, Ostrom asked to look at one of the very rare specimens of *Archaeopteryx lithographica* (pronounced ar-kee-op-ter-icks lith-o-grafika), the oldest known bird. *Archaeopteryx* was described by Hermann von Meyer in 1861 and is now known from seven specimens (and a single feather) from prehistoric coral atoll lagoons found in Bavaria in rocks of the latest Jurassic age, about 145 million years ago.

Archaeopteryx had typical flight feathers on both wing and tail. It could fly, but probably not very well. When examining it very closely, he found an exact match in shape of all the bone joints with those of *Deinonychus*. Every single bone is exactly similar in shape to those of the Maniraptorans. Ostrom's drawing of *Archaeopteryx* shows it in a running pose to illustrate the similarity to dinosaurs. It is likely that birds arose from the Maniraptorans in the late Jurassic. *Deinonychus* is one example of an animal that links dinosaurs with birds.

Learning to Fly One Step at a Time

The young eagles we enjoyed watching practice their flying come at the task from a different perspective than their predecessors. Eagles and other modern raptors are pushed from the nest into the air itself. They must fly to survive.

Earlier raptors started the task from a safer position, with the terra firma underfoot. They used their arms, covered with small feathers, to run faster. The grabbing stroke of the arms in running Maniraptorans is exactly the same as the power stroke in bird flight.

Feathers on the arm and hand added the thrust of grabbing to their running speed, allowing them to catch prey and giving *Archaeopteryx* the ability to run its way into flight.

After *Archaeopteryx*, birds became more modern very rapidly. They grew a horny beak and lost their teeth, bones became hollow, the front several tail vertebrae were included in the hipbones, and the other tail vertebrae were greatly shortened. All of these measures saved weight. The easiest way to go faster (or save energy) is to lose weight. They also added more muscle power to the wing stroke, greatly increasing the size of what we call the breast of the bird.

All of these changes occurred more than 130 million ago, and are documented at the site in northeast China. There we find modernized birds (but still with teeth) as well as some of their dinosaur Maniraptoran cousins with feathers, that could not fly. By this time birds had certainly spread all over the world, including this area, but their remains were not preserved here.

This "new improved" dinosaur seems to work pretty well, at least after the young ones soar beyond the steep learning curve of flight training. Perhaps fledglings will still be leaping awkwardly out of nests 100 million years from now.

Bald eagles

Wild turkey

National Birdhood: Eagle? Or Turkey?

By Marc Hequet

B ald eagles, our national symbol since 1776, adorn currency, biker gear, rear windows of pickup trucks and all other things patriotic. Yet no less a figure than Benjamin Franklin backed wild turkeys as the best choice for national birdhood.

Which bird deserves it — turkeys? Or eagles? Both birds are back in numbers along the Mississippi River and elsewhere. Shall we take up this debate?

Sports teams may call themselves "eagles." Disappointed fans may call them "turkeys." *Meleagris gallopavo*, the North American

Big River Magazine, July-August 2009

bird, was called a "turkey" in England as early as 1555, and often was the main course at Christmas dinner. People thought it was a species of guinea fowl imported from Madagascar by way of Turkey.

To be sure, the North American turkey's coloration is promising for a U.S. national bird — brownish red, a little white, maybe even some blue, with an iridescent sheen. The bald eagle, on the other hand, is black and white. Does that tell us anything?

Turkeys aren't above patriotism. I saw one stalking a car — a Honda — at Minnehaha Park in Minneapolis in April. It strutted around the sedan and then began pecking the bumper. A big guy on the driver's side got out and waved his arms. The bird, little impressed, retreated two steps.

Turkeys do stand their ground. A big tom blocked my way on a Mississippi River bike trail last autumn. Didn't budge. Looked me in the eye as I warily peddled around it.

Are they fearless? In May, a turkey crashed through the window of a house in the small town of Mishicot, in northeast Wisconsin. A woman and her five-year-old daughter fled to a bedroom. Mom counterattacked, opening two outside doors. The turkey, prowling the kitchen, went out one of them.

Eagles stay out of houses, as far as we know. They take fish alive or dead, but eat whatever they want, including roadkill deer. An immature great blue heron as well as baby and adult ducks have been found in eagle nests. If an eagle wants a baby bird, I don't know what anybody could do to stop it.

In short, neither candidate for national birdhood behaves in ways in keeping with the high calling of the office. Perhaps most damaging of all are lax parenting skills.

Bill Route is an ecologist with the National Park Service, based in Ashland, Wis., who monitors wildlife and other resources in nine national parks. He hires wildlife biologists who are also arborists — professional climbers — to climb trees, inspect eagle aeries and remove eaglets for blood tests that check for environmental contaminants. Eagles eat what lives in the water and so are great indicators of water quality. Of course, after the blood is drawn, climbers go back up the tree to return the young to their nest.

What happens when adult birds catch science in the act? You've seen eagles up close at the National Eagle Center in Wabasha, Minn. — hooked beaks, powerful talons. "They certainly have the weapons," admits Route.

Yet eagles don't attack the climbers who invade their nests and carry off their young. "Bald eagles are not very aggressive," Route adds. "I wouldn't call them docile. They'll fly around the nest and squawk and maybe sit on a branch nearby, but they won't swoop down on a climber."

In contrast, climbers entering nests of goshawks must watch out for returning adults, which attack viciously.

What about turkeys? They nest on the ground. Mother turkeys defend their nests, sometimes chasing away hawks and other predators. On the other hand, they routinely lays eggs in the nests of other species.

Males? Forget it. They provide no parenting.

The *Peoria (Ill.) Journal Star* reported May 30 that earlier in the spring, one Dave Scifres found a wild turkey nest in Tazewell County, Ill., while mushroom hunting. The enterprising fellow set up a trail camera. It shot many images of raccoons, including one of a raccoon eating a turkey egg. Where was Mom?

Turkey? Eagle?

"Having seen both of them," muses Route, "I think I would still go for the bald eagle. I think they are pretty majestic."

Both birds, however, are authentic independents. They do what they do with no consideration for human ideals or national interests. Whatever we read into their appearance or behavior isn't about them — it's about us.

So now you know more about turkeys and eagles — and possibly less about national values. In any case, let the record show that both turkeys and eagles can fly — not the case for either animal symbolizing our top political parties.

Contributors

Pamela Eyden wrote 24 of the stories in this book, including "Turning a No-Man's Land into a Nature Preserve." She is *Big River Magazine*'s editor-at-large.

Marc Hequet wrote "National Birdhood: Eagle? or Turkey?" He is a freelance writer who lives in St. Paul.

Fran Howard wrote "Back to the Bluffs." She is a freelance writer specializing in wildlife and conservation stories who lives in St. Paul.

Thomas V. Lerczak wrote "Haunts of the Red-headed Woodpecker" and "Swallows of the Upper Mississippi." The former employee of the Illinois Nature Preserves Commission and the Illinois Natural History Survey is the author of *Side Channels: A Collection of Nature Writing and Memoir.* He lives near the Illinois River.

Molly McGuire wrote "Nighthawk Twilight" and "Listen for These White Swans' Songs." She is *Big River Magazine*'s managing editor.

Reggie McLeod co-wrote "Looking Just Ducky." He is *Big River Magazine*'s editor and publisher.

Joan Schnabel wrote six of the stories in this book, including "Kestrels — Little Raptors with a Big Attitude." She is a physician and bird educator with a raptor permit from the USFWS who lives in Iowa City, Iowa.

Robert E. Sloan wrote "Soaring with the Dinosaurs." The former professor of paleontology at the University of Minnesota for 44 years lives in Winona, Minn.

Sally Sloan wrote "Scrappy Eagles on a Blue Water Day." The former professor of mathematics lives near Winona, Minn.

Alan Stankevitz is a wildlife photographer who specializes in birds and lives in La Crescent, Minn.

Tom Watson wrote "Paddling for Birds on the Mississippi." The author of numerous outdoor guides lives in Appleton, Wis.

Index

A

accipiter 117
Accipitridae 117
Ad Hoc Eastern Population Tundra Swan Committee 85
aerial swan counts 85, 179–180
aerial waterfowl surveys 181
Aghaming Park 71–75
Alaska 24, 83, 86, 101
Allamakee County 44
Alliant Power Plant 41
Alma, Wis. 38, 42, 85
American crows 106–110
American kestrels 68, 120–123
American Museum of Natural History 188
American white pelicans 78–82
Anderson, Bob 37, 39–42, 43–45
Angell, Tony 110
Appalachian Trail 72
Archaeopteryx 186–187
Archaeopteryx lithographica 190
Arctic peregrines 41
Ardea 13
Ardea herodias 7
Army Road 176
arrowhead 85, 184
Ashland, Wis. 194
Audubon Society 8, 15, 123
    Coulee Region 28, 143
    Dubuque, Iowa 141
    Quad City 145
Ause, Bruce 53
Australia 5, 30

B

backwater birding 165–169
bald eagles 32–45, 35–49, 107, 143–144, 157–158, 172, 192–195
bank swallows 125–126
Baraboo Hills 53
Baraboo, Wis. 18
Barn Bluff 53
barn owls 148
barn swallows 127–128
barred owls 55, 65–69, 72, 144, 146–147

bass 94
Battle Creek Regional Park 173
Bay City, Wis. 173
Bayport, Minn. 39, 43
Beaver Island 10
Bell Museum 7
belted kingfishers 2–5, 126
Bertom Lake 175
Bettendorf, Iowa 176
Big Marsh 174
binoculars 167
Birder's World 72, 163
birding from a kayak 165–169
birding in fall 171–178
    Bertom Lake 175
    Black Hawk Park 175
    Eagle Point Park 176
    Effigy Mounds National Monument 175
    Goose Island Park 174
    Lake Pepin 173
    Lock and Dam 14 Eagle Area 176
    Long Lake Canoe Trail 174
    Mines of Spain State Recreation Area 176
    Nelson Dewey State Park 175
    New Albin, Iowa 176
    Trempealeau National Wildlife Refuge 173
    Turkey River Bottoms 175
    Wyalusing State Park 175
    Yellow River State Forest 175
birding in winter 139–145
    Coulee Region 143
    E.B. Lyons Nature Center 142
    Goose Island 143
    Pikes Peak State Park 142
Birds of North America 28, 111
blackbirds 21–26
black-crowned night herons 27
black ducks 134
Black Hawk Park 175
black terns 73
black vultures 48
blue herons. See great blue herons
blue-winged teal 133–135
Bluffton, Iowa 43
Boehm, Karla 69
boreal owls 148
BP Deep Water Horizon oil spill

effects on pelicans 82
Breeding Bird Census 72
Breeding Bird Survey 163
Britton, Ed 81–82
broad-winged hawks 177
Brown, Charles R. 126
brown-headed nuthatches 30
Brown, Mary Bomberger 127
Brownsville, Minn. 85, 172
Buena Vista Park 173
Buffalo County, Wis. 44, 73
buffleheads 171
bull-bats. See nighthawks
burrowing owls 67
Buteo lineatus 61

C

caddisflies 23
California brown pelicans 80
Canada 3, 24, 47, 83, 86, 100–101, 104, 108, 113
Canada geese 182
canvasbacks 89, 102–104, 135, 175, 182
canvasbacks in flight 136
Carlisle, Kathleen 18
Carter, Carol 113
Cassville, Wis. 38, 43–44, 175
Castle Rock Cliff 44
Cathartes 48
Cathartes aura 52
cattle egrets 81
Cedar River 64
cedar waxwings 152
cerulean warblers 72, 162–163
Chesapeake Bay 86
chickadees 139, 141
chicken hawks 61–64, 118
chimney swift 124
Chippewa National Forest 172
chipping sparrow 174
Chordeiles minor 111
cliff swallows 126–127
climate change
    kestrels 123
    tundra swans 86
Clinton, Iowa 10, 81, 85
closed areas 184–185
Cohasset, Minn. 43
common nighthawks 73, 105, 111–115
Connecticut 114
Coon Rapids Dam Regional Park 173
Cooper's hawks 116–119
coraciiformes 5
Cormorant Island 81

cormorants. See double-crested cormorants
Cornell Lab of Ornithology 109, 111
Corvus 108
    brachyrhynchos 108
    corax 108
Costa Rica 24
counting waterfowl 181–185
Crane Count 18
Crawford County, Wis. 44
crossbills 145
crows 107–110, 151
    language 110
    tools 109
Custer, Christine 8–10, 13–15
Custer, Thomas 14

D

dabblers 132, 134
Dakotas 81, 83, 90
Darwin, Charles 30
Davenport, Iowa 25, 145
Davis, Jim 4–5
DDT 10, 37, 43, 95–96, 119, 122–123, 178
Decorah, Iowa 39
Deinonychus 190
Delta Farm News 95
Diamond Bluff, Wis. 167
Ding Darling National Wildlife Refuge 13
dinosaurs 187–191
    bird behaviors 188
    Deinonychus fossil 189
    development of feathers 189
    distinctive vocal calls 188
    raptors 189
diving ducks 135, 137, 145, 183
Dodson, Peter 188
double-crested cormorants 30, 49, 81, 92–97, 177, 182
downy woodpeckers 59, 140
dragonflies 21, 164
drawdowns 85, 184
Dubuque, Iowa 176
duck hunting 133
Ducks Unlimited 90
Duluth, Minn. 47, 69, 114

E

eagle nest 187–188
Eagle Point Park 176
eagles 33–34, 182, 187–191. See also bald eagles
    flight feathers 188
eastern bluebirds 60

eastern brown pelicans 80
eastern kingbirds 150–152
eastern screech owls 144, 148
Effigy Mounds National Monument 37, 175
egret plumes 8, 14
egrets 8, 28
    cattle 13
    great 13
    habitat loss 14
    little 13
    reddish 13
    snowy 11
Egyptian vultures 30
Elk River, Minn. 167
European starlings 60
evolution of flight 187–191

F

Faber, Ray 14
fall birding
    cormorants 174
    hawks 175
    tundra swans 175
fall migration 177–178
    broad-winged hawks 177
    canvasbacks 177
    double-crested cormorants 177
    ospreys 177
    semipalmated sandpipers 177
    snow geese 177
    trumpeter swans 178
    turkey vultures 178
Ferryville, Wis. 172
fingernail clams 184
Fisher, Pat 141
fish-hawks. *See* ospreys
floodplain forest 10, 57, 61–62, 64, 73–75, 128
Florida 13, 15, 19, 53
Forestville State Park 48
foxes 90
Franklin, Benjamin 193
Friends of Pool 9 49
frog hawks 61–64

G

gadwalls 134
Galapagos 30
Galena, Ill. 91
Galli, Joan 9
Genoa, Wis. 85
Georgia 53
Gibson, Marge 51, 68

Gifts of the Crow 110
Gillette, Laurence 113
gizzard shad 94, 157
golden eagles 49
goldeneyes 89
golden shiners 94
Gomer's Island 81
Gonzo the non-vomiting vulture 51–54
Goose Island Park 174
great blue herons 6–10, 11, 13, 27–28, 81
great egrets 11–15, 12, 81
greater sandhill cranes 17–20
greater scaup 101, 183
great gray owls 67–69, 148
great horned owls 37–38, 42, 48, 62, 65–69, 71,
        108, 144, 147–149, 151
Great River Bluff State Park 38
Great Spirit Bluff 44
green herons 27–30
green-winged teal 99–100, 133–134
Guttenberg, Iowa 175

H

Hanover, Ill. 91
harriers 143
Hastings, Minn. 9, 25
hawking 58
Hawkins, Tex 23
Hawk Mountain 53
Hawk Ridge 47
hawks 172
Henderson, Carrol 28–29
Hennepin County 172
Hennepin County Parks 178
herons 7–10, 13–15, 80
    black-crowned night heron 27
    great blue 7–10, 27–28
    green 27–30
    habitat loss 14
    little blue 13
    tricolored 13
Hixon Forest Nature Center 174
Homer, Minn. 43, 187
hooded mergansers 176
Hoogland, John L. 126
hopscotch migration 53
horned larks 141
Horner, Jack 188
house wrens 128
Houston, Minn. 48, 69, 148
Houston Nature Center 69
Hudson Bay 83
Hwy. 35 between Ferryville and Lynxville, Wis.

I

Illinois 17, 19, 57, 59
Illinois River 127
Indiana 19, 114
Ingold, Danny J. 60
International Crane Foundation 18–20
International Festival of Owls 69, 148
International Migratory Bird Day 15, 164
International Owl Center 48, 148
Intriguing Owls 148
Iowa 17, 19, 37
Iowa City, Iowa 52

J

Jackson, Dan 143
Japan 28
Japanese hops 75
Jeffers, Carl 95
John A. Latsch State Park 38, 44
Johnsgard, Paul A. 148
juncoes 131, 141–142

K

Kellogg Weaver Dunes Scientific and Natural
    Area 173
Kennedy, Mike 134–135, 139
Keokuk, Iowa 62, 126
Kester, Dave 41
kestrels 120–123
kettle 177
kingfishers 3–5, 142
Kinstler, Karla 48–49
Knutson, Melinda 25

L

Lacey Act 15
La Crescent, Minn. 44
La Crosse, Wis. 8, 13, 25, 28, 38, 97
Lake Okeechobee 48
Lake Onalaska 97, 177, 182
Lake Ontario 93
Lake Pepin 44, 172
Lansing, Iowa 38–39, 49
Last Child in the Woods 139
Latsch Island 72–74
Latsch, John 73
Lesher, Fred 8, 28
Lewis, Steve 97

Lima, Peru 42
little blue herons 13
Little Galloo Island 93
long-eared owls 67–69, 144, 148
Long Lake Canoe Trail 174
Loring Park 108
Louisiana 13
Louv, Richard 139
Lynxville, Wis. 43–44

M

Maassen's Bluff 44
Maiden Rock 44
Maiden Rock, Wis. 38, 43
Mallard Capital of the World 91
Mallard Festival 91
mallards 72, 88–91, 100, 104, 133, 182
Maniraptors 190
Manitoba 90
maps of the river 167
Marquette, Iowa 37
Maryland 114
Marzluff, John 109, 110
mayflies 23, 28, 48, 111, 127
McCay, Kelly 25
McGowan, Kevin 109
McGregor, Iowa 62, 142
mercury in peregrines 41
mergansers 171, 173
merlins 121
Merritt, Dixon Lanier 80
Mertes Slough 10
Mexico 24, 71, 100
Michigan 90
migration 181–185
    flocking 25–26
    grand passage 137
    strategies 23–26
migration through Upper Mississippi 183
    bald eagles 157–158
    blackbirds 25
    Canada geese 137
    changes in the river 183
    chimney swifts 161
    ducks 133–137, 145
    golden eagles 145
    locks and dams 183
    ospreys 158
    purple martins 161
    rough legged hawks 142
    swallows 161
    tundra swans 83–87, 137
migratory water birds 182–185

Mines of Spain State Recreation Area 176
mink 91
Minneapolis 108
Minnesota 3, 17, 19, 37, 81, 83
Minnesota Department of Natural Resources 9,
        28, 44
Minnesota Land Trust 44
Minnesota Valley National Wildlife Refuge 173
Mississippi flyway 85, 165, 171
Mississippi River Companion 167
Moline, Ill. 25
Mollie Kestrel 121–123
Montana 81, 189
Montana State University 188
Monticello to Elk River, Minn. 172
mosquitoes 8, 23, 57, 111, 163
Mount Hosmer 49
Muscatine, Iowa 62

N

National Audubon Society 62
national bird 193–195
National Eagle Center 145, 194
National Park Service 167, 194
National Wildlife Refuges 15
Nebraska 126
Nelson Dewey State Park 175
Nelson, Eric 10, 14, 182–185
New Albin, Iowa 176
Newberry, Gretchen 114
New Caledonian crow 30, 109
New Hampshire 114
New Jersey 83, 114
New York 114
Niabi Zoo Conservation Science Center 25
nighthawks 73, 105, 111–115
nighthawk survey 2001 113–114
night herons 73
nightjar 111
night roosts 144
Norell, Mark 188
North America 11
North American Owls, Biology and Natural
        History 148
northern hawk owls 69, 148
northern saw-whet owls 148
northern shovelers 100, 134
Northern States Power Plant 39
Nosek, John 14
Nunavut 83
nuthatches 140, 143

O

O'Connor, Julie 47
Ohio 4, 19, 90
oldest known bird 190
olive-backed oriole 5
Olson, Pete 39–42
Omaha, Neb. 42
ospreys 73, 155–156, 158, 177
Ostrom, John 189–190
owl festivals 69
owl migration 67
owls in winter 65–69, 147–148

P

paddling for birds 165–169
Panama 5
Partavia airplane 182
Partners in Flight 164
Peabody Museum 189
Pelican Island, Fla. 15
Pelican Island, Ill. 81
pelicans 49, 97, 182
Pennsylvania 53
Pepin County, Wis. 44
peregrine falcons 31, 36–45, 122
pesticides 95, 114. See also DDT
Peterson, Minn. 51
pied-billed grebes 101–103
Pierce County, Wis. 44
Pigs Eye Island 9
pike 94
pileated woodpeckers 72, 138, 142, 145, 153–155
pintails 134, 171
Pocosin Wildlife Refuge 86
Pool 4 181, 184
Pool 5 85, 184
Pool 5a 85
Pool 7 182
Pool 8 85, 180, 184
Pool 9 49, 175, 177, 183
Pool 10 62
Pool 13 81, 185
pools 1 through 14
        rookeries 10, 14
pools 4, 5 and 5a 85
pools 4 through 11
        swans 87
pools 4 through 13 182
pools 7, 8, 9 and 13
        canvasbacks 135
pools 7 through 9 85, 184
Prairie du Chien, Wis. 175
Prairie Island, Winona, Minn. 173
prothonotary warblers 72

puddle ducks 134, 183
purple martins 128, 129

Q

Quad Cities 25, 167
Queen's Bluff 38, 42, 44

R

raccoons 37–38, 62
Raddatz Rock Shelter 53
Raptor Center 49
Raptor Education Group Inc. 68
Raptor Resource Project 37, 39–43
ravens 108, 110
red-bellied woodpeckers 59
red eyes in birds 118
red-headed woodpeckers 56–60, 145
redhorse 94
red-shouldered hawks 61–64, 70–75, 175
red-tailed hawks 62–64, 68, 91, 148
red-winged blackbirds 21–26. See blackbirds
Red Wing, Minn. 9, 44, 53, 85
reed canary grass 75
REGI 68
Rendell, Wallace B. 128
Rep. Peterson, Collin 93–97
Reynolds, Chris 24
Ries, Amy 41
ring-billed gulls 93
ring-necked ducks 135, 171
River Bird Blog 72
Robertson, Raleigh J. 128
Rochester, Minn. 41, 108
Rock Island, Ill. 14, 145
rookeries 14
Roosevelt, President Theodore 15
rough-legged hawks 141–143
rough-winged swallows 124–126, 128
Route, Bill 194
ruby-throated hummingbirds 57
rusty blackbirds 72

S

Sabula, Iowa 8
Saginaw Bay, Michigan 93
sago pondweed 85
Saint Mary's University 14
sandhill cranes 16–20, 154–155, 168
saw-whet owls 67
Sax-Zim Bog 69, 148
Sayles, Dick 145

screech owls 65–69
semipalmated sandpiper 177
semipalmated sandpipers 170, 178
Sherman, Paul W. 126
shoebill storks 80
short-eared owls 148
Sibley's Guide to Birds 101, 104
Sky Kennels 41
Smithsonian Institution 5
snags 128
snakes 62
snow buntings 141
snow geese 177
snowy egrets 11
snowy owls 69, 148
solitary sandpipers 168
South America 113
South Carolina 83
South Dakota 19
sparrow hawks 122
Spoon River 127
Spring Lake 185
St. Cloud, Minn. 4
St. Croix River 39, 43
Stefanski, Mary 75
Stemper, Brian 133–134
Stewards of the Upper Mississippi River Refuge
    81
Stockholm, Wis. 173
St. Paul 9, 49
Stravers, Jon 62–64
suckers 94
swallows 72, 125–129
    bank 125–127
    barn 127–128
    cliff 126–127
    purple martin 128
    rough-winged 125–126, 128
    tree 127–128
Swan Research Program 86
swans. See tundra swans, trumpeter swans
Swanson, Richie 71–75, 163

T

teal 133–134, 182
Tekiela, Stan 148
Texas 13, 19
Thomson, Ill. 81
Thrune, Bill 182
Tierra del Fuego 47
tree sparrows 141, 143
tree swallows 127–128, 160–161
Trempealeau County, Wis. 18, 44

Trempealeau National Wildlife Refuge 73, 75, 157, 173
Trempealeau, Wis. 85, 167
trichamonis 118
trumpeter swans 86, 172, 178
Tschirgi, Matt 142
tufted titmice 143
tundra swans 77, 83–84, 172, 178, 180, 182–185
Turkey River Bottoms 175
turkey vultures 46–54, 57, 175–176, 178
    migration 53–54
Twin Cities 167

U

University of Minnesota 7
University of Minnesota Raptor Center 155, 158
University of Pennsylvania 188
University of South Dakota 114
University of Washington 109
Upper Iowa River 64
Upper Mississippi National Wildlife and Fish Refuge 14, 73–75, 85, 133, 181
    Savanna District 81
Upper Mississippi River Campaign 62
Upper Mississippi River Refuge. See Upper Mississippi National Wildlife and Fish Refuge
Upper Mississippi Science Center 8
U.S. Department of Agriculture 95
U.S. Fish and Wildlife Service (USFWS) 10, 19, 51, 72, 85, 90, 94, 167, 182–185
U.S. Geological Survey 183
    Breeding Bird Survey 57
    Northern Prairie Research Center 3
    Upper Midwest Environmental Sciences Center 13, 25

V

Venezuela 53
Vermillion River Bottoms 9
Vermont 114
von Meyer, Hermann 190
vultures. See turkey vultures

W

Wabasha, Minn. 62, 85, 167, 194
Wapsipinicon River 64
warblers 73
Waterbirds journal 14
waterfowl counts 183–185
waterfowl migration 133–137
Watertown, New York 93

Waukon Junction, Iowa 44
Weaver Bottoms 85
Weaver, Minn. 140
West Bluff 44
West Nile virus 123
West Wisconsin Land Trust 44
wetland loss 90
whip-poor-wills 111
whistling swans. See tundra swans
Whistling Wings 91
white-breasted nuthatches 140, 143
white pelicans 166, 167
Whitman Dam 85
wigeons 134, 182
wild celery 85, 175, 177, 184
wild turkeys 193–195
willowleaf beetles 159
Winona Bird Club 74
Winona, Minn. 10, 23, 38, 42, 73, 85, 181
Winter Birding Festival 69
Wisconsin 3, 17, 19, 37, 48, 53, 74, 90
Wisconsin Department of Natural Resources 74–75, 158
Wisconsin Islands Closed Area 85
wood ducks 98, 104, 133–134, 134, 182
woodpecker finches 30
Woodruff's Island 81
Wyalusing State Park 175

Y

yellow-headed blackbirds 73
Yellow River State Forest 175

Z

Zarwell, Ric 49
zugunruhe 172

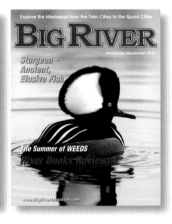